PROMETHEAN PIRATE

PROMETHEAN PIRATE

JASON REZA JORJANI

ARKTOS
LONDON 2022

ISBN 978-1-915755-01-8 (Paperback)
978-1-915755-02-5 (Hardback)
978-1-915755-03-2 (Ebook)

EDITING Constantin von Hoffmeister

COVER & LAYOUT Tor Westman

Arktos.com fb.com/Arktos @arktosmedia arktosmedia

CONTENTS

"A dozen or so who are tomorrow's leading men and women? They are the finest minds, don't forget, eliminated from the running. Come now, David, I think that's a pretty fair return from a minimum outlay. It's far better than expensive spying systems, pinching penny secrets which are out of date by the time you get them back to Moscow. No, no, no, no, this is a long-term investment. You pinpoint your best minds, the coming men, and make sure that they never arrive."

— Anthony Price, *The Alamut Ambush* (1971)

CHAPTER 1

INCENDIARY IDEAS

LOOKING BACK on my life, there is one thing that I have absolutely no regrets about, namely the pursuit of Philosophy as my life's calling. At the age of forty-one, a little over twenty years after fully committing myself to this path, I have succeeded in becoming a philosopher. That really is saying a lot, since one of the first things that I realized in the course of studying Philosophy was that there are hardly any philosophers left. "One of" the first things, because the *very first* thing that I realized is that Philosophy is the highest or most fundamental pursuit to which a person can dedicate him- or herself. As integral thought that generates or discovers concepts in the domains of ontology, epistemology, ethics, politics, and aesthetics, Philosophy, in the proper sense of the word, both transcends and undergirds all of the sciences and the arts, including political science. On this definition of Philosophy, at which I had arrived by the time I was in college at NYU, there have not been more than two dozen philosophers in all of recorded history. Moreover, Philosophy in this integral and legitimate sense has so degenerated in the past several decades that, in my generation and the one preceding my own, there have perhaps been only a handful of actual philosophers on the face of the Earth. To have succeeded in becoming one of them by the midpoint of my expected lifespan is, then, no mean accomplishment.

Plato, Aristotle, Kant, Hegel, Nietzsche, Heidegger, Sartre — whatever one thinks of their particular ideas, or whichever of them one prefers to the others, these are the kinds of men that epitomize existence in the modality of the philosopher. In my view, lamentably, they *have* almost exclusively been *men*. Much as I have sung the praises of Hypatia of Alexandria and recognized her as a martyr, there is no indication that she was a philosopher any more than Simone de Beauvoir or Hannah Arendt were philosophers. To Arendt's credit, she *knew* that she wasn't a philosopher and made this quite clear, limiting herself, like Leo Strauss, to the claim of being a "political thinker." By contrast, Hypatia was not a philosopher because, as far as we know, in her capacity as a Neo-Pythagorean teacher in the Platonist Academy of Alexandria, she had no political philosophy to speak of. In fact, as far as I can tell, the *only* female philosopher whose writings are extant is Ayn Rand. Howsoever one might assess her positions or her personality, quite apart from the *content* of her work, the *form* of her voluminous writing and of her Herculean intellectual life is that of a philosopher in the proper sense.

Anyone who tries to claim that Madame Blavatsky or Savitri Devi are "female philosophers" is an ignoramus with shit for brains. I do apologize for mentioning these two women in the same sentence, though, because I actually have a lot of respect and admiration for Helena Blavatsky, including for that trickster aspect of her personality that got her branded as a charlatan. She was my kind of woman, and I would love to have known her. A cosmopolitan New Yorker, no less, at the peak of her career. The Hitler-worshipping Traditionalist Hindu "Savitri Devi," on the other hand, is what a brain tumor looks like when it gets hold of a pen and bleeds itself out on reams of wasted paper. In any case, neither of them developed or discovered concepts that cut across the full spectrum of the domains of properly philosophical thought, from ontology and epistemology to ethics, politics, and aesthetics.

Although the nineteenth and twentieth centuries produced the greatest number of philosophers of any epoch in the history of Philosophy, the early nineteenth century does mark the beginning of the degeneration or decomposition of Philosophy, and by the end of the twentieth century Philosophy had entered such a terminal decline that the greatest thinker of the century, namely Martin Heidegger, explicitly wrote of "the end of Philosophy." Albeit, in my view, prematurely. But Heidegger was right to identify the essential problem as a decomposition of Philosophy into the disparate empirical sciences and, conversely, the deracination of empirical science from its necessary foundation in philosophical thought. Beginning with Physics in the early 1800s, and then continuing with Biology (and Biochemistry) in the late 1800s, and Psychology as well as the Social and Political Sciences in the early 1900s, practitioners of the sciences pursued a path of specialization that, unbeknown to them, was also a path to bastardization. They became cuckold bastards watching their forlorn mother, Sophia, be gang-raped by atheistic materialism and religious traditionalism.

Insisting that Philosophy retain its integrity as a discipline that is devoted to thinking both beneath and beyond the specialized frameworks of the distinct sciences that decomposed from out of it is not some arbitrary demand. When the sciences become uprooted from Philosophy, and philosophers are no longer recognized as the most fundamental and far-reaching thinkers, scientific research gets stuck within one or another paradigm that misrepresents itself as a mirror of objective reality. At the same time, politics is reduced to a battle between ideologies, whose partisans are incapable of reflectively questioning the ontological and epistemological foundations of their ethical and political positions. This is because they are ideologues or, worse yet, academic critics of ideologues, rather than philosophers capable of thinking politically — as Plato and Aristotle thought politically by extension of contemplating the nature of existence, the basic principles of cosmology, and the structure of knowledge.

Not only does such a destruction of coherent philosophical thought serve to entrench the exclusionary hegemony of the idiotic materialist paradigm that has warped the progress of modern science, it also serves to protect religious traditionalism from the revolutionary threat that dogmatic religion has always faced from the philosopher. Whether it is the schools of Pythagoras torched by the conservative mobs of Sicily, the execution of Socrates by the Athenian democracy, Plato's nearly lethal misadventure at Syracuse, Aristotle's self-exile from Athens, the Caliphate's execution of Shahab al-din Sohrevardi, or the burning of Giordano Bruno at the stake by the Roman Catholic Church, the philosopher has always been a heretic — or even an apostate — by *nature.* Jean-Jacques Rousseau aptly recognized this when he argued that the execution of Socrates was justified, and that there should only ever be a "national philosophy" in line with the "civic religion" that forms the basis of the "general will" of one or another democratic civil society. This brings us to another unpleasant point, namely that serious philosophical thought — even, or maybe especially, when it has ferociously defended Liberty — has almost always been opposed to democracy. As Plato already understood in his Allegory of the Cave, the majority of "the people" do not want to think, and they so violently resent those who make them think that the masses are willing to murder anyone who sets out to enlighten them by breaking the chains of their ignorance.

A philosophical position on the meaning and purpose of Philosophy is referred to as a "Metaphilosophy." The foregoing discussion can, consequently, be considered a summary of what I call a "Prometheist Metaphilosophy." In other words, a concept of what Philosophy is in the first place, which motivates and grounds the various philosophical concepts integral to the "Prometheist" way of thinking that I have developed since *Prometheus and Atlas* (Arktos 2016), which was written in 2012 and published in 2016. I am by no means the first thinker to associate Prometheus with the task of the philosopher. Karl Marx and Martin Heidegger have respectively been identified as intellectual godfathers of two of the most radically opposed ideological orientations in the twentieth century, namely Marxist Communism and National Socialism, but Marx and Heidegger shared this assessment of Prometheus. Both men saw this titanic trickster as the archetypal or proto-typical "philosopher" and, by extension, as the patron deity of the sciences that disintegrated from out of Philosophy. If there is a particular specter that can be associated with the spectrality of the worldwide Communist revolution that Marx heralded, it is Prometheus, whose praises Marx reverently sings in his early writings. As for Heidegger, besides acknowledging Prometheus as the first philosopher and scientist in his Rectoral Address (in a manner of speaking, of course, such that he sees the tragedies of Aeschylus as the *Abgrund* [abyss] from out of which Pre-Socratic Philosophy emerges), as I argued in *Prometheus and Atlas*, I am convinced that when Heidegger ended up saying that merely human meditations or endeavors would no longer suffice to face the challenge of world-enframing technologies, it is Prometheus that he had in mind when he claimed that "only a god can save us now."

A Prometheist Metaphilosophy is, then, a vision of the purpose of Philosophy that defends the philosopher's position as an inventive rebel against whatever has become an unreflectively oppressive established order. By discovering or creating new concepts through irreverent questioning and bold exploration, the philosopher dethrones gods and other tyrants—including a tyrannous majority—who enforce ignorance, in order to break the chains of societal stagnation with disruptive innovation. Like a thief he breaks into places that are off limits, and there is something of an arsonist in him. He brings fire!

Concepts are complex but coherent ideas that allow for an organization of information and experience. Concepts need to be properly differentiated from mere notions, or intuitions, as well as from variables, theories, hypotheses, and beliefs or dogmas. Most people outside of the discipline of Philosophy ignorantly conflate these terms with one another. Meanwhile, even within the discipline, a majority of academic "professors of Philosophy" (who should never be confused with philosophers) have rejected concept formation as the task of the philosopher. I will come back around to comment on this catastrophe, but first, what is a concept?

Mere notions or intuitions do not have sufficient scope and internal structure to be considered concepts, nor are instances of the relevance of these ideas as clearly identifiable as instantiations of a philosophical concept. That "might makes right" is a mere notion or intuition, but, aside from the fact that it is extremely vague, one would be hard-pressed to identify unambiguous historical or experiential examples of this idea. After all, as Martin Luther King famously said, "... the arc of the moral universe is long, but it bends toward justice." So, for example, while a certain regime or a particular dictator seems to have gotten away with one or another use of force to achieve an objective, from a historical standpoint it is always possible that there will be some kind of retrospective or retroactive justice that would alter this assessment. Of course, King's statement is also nothing more than a vague notion or intuition. It certainly falls far short of any philosophical concept of a purposive history, let alone one with an overarching moral aim (*telos*). In contrast to "might makes right," Nietzsche's "Will to Power" is a philosophical concept. Implicit in this concept is a certain understanding of "will" and of "power" as well as their respective relationships to "truth" claims and to the nature of "life." It has relevance on the level of ontology, epistemology, and psychology (the intersection of aesthetics and ethics), as well as socio-political implications (including profound consequences for the social phenomenon of religion).

This does not, however, mean that the Will to Power is a scientific hypothesis or a theory. A hypothesis is an assumption about some aspect of nature that can be tested by means of disciplined observation and rigorous experimentation. By contrast, a theory is a framework of principles or law-like formulations arrived at on the basis of analysis of extensive data produced by experiments devised to test one or more hypotheses. While Nietzsche was acutely aware of Charles Darwin's theory of evolution by the natural selection of random mutations and is constructively critiquing Darwin's theory with his concept of the Will to Power, this concept itself is neither a hypothesis nor a theory.

In fact, the Will to Power is a concept that is more fundamental than any scientific theory, since it conceptualizes why the truth claims of any scientific endeavor are really made and how such claims actually function to set up or restructure a certain configuration of power relations. Even at the level of paradigms, science can never evaluate the adequacy of Nietzsche's concept of the Will to Power. Rather, Nietzsche's concept helps us to evaluate science and its actual place in society and meaning for life—despite what scientists would prefer to believe. Science is not the most fundamental form of thought. Philosophy is. When scientists lose sight of this, they get stuck in unquestioned paradigms, which will continue to be self-validating by pushing to the forbidden fringe of experience all phenomena that do not fit the mold of the theories within that paradigm. At the bottom of paradigms, such as the Cartesian paradigm, are philosophical concepts that more fundamentally define things like space and time.

Another major difference between theories and concepts is that scientific descriptions, including predictive ones, consist of compound propositions that are constituted by distinct variables that can be removed or substituted in order to transform or redefine equations. Philosophical concepts are more integral than that. They have a certain endo-consistency. While distinct facets or elements can be discerned within a certain concept, such as "will" and "power" and the respective relation of each to "truth" and "life" within the concept of the Will to Power, a concept cannot be pulled apart in such a way that some part of it can be replaced or substituted while it remains the same concept.

It can certainly be the case that, over time, most people (from amongst those who are even capable of grasping the concept in the first place) come to the conclusion that a certain concept, while perfectly coherent, has no real-world application or is not consonant with our broadening or deepening experience (including historical experience). For example, this might be said of Kant's Categorical Imperative. It was far more compelling before Darwinian evolution and the two world wars. Or scientific research in Biology, including into the way that morphic resonance or formative causation actually work, might render Plato's conception of the *eidos* or "forms" less relevant to our domain of experience. It will not, however, have "disproved" the concept or created conditions for a restructuring of the concept along the lines that a scientific theory might be restructured to accommodate further relevant data. The internal logical cohesion of a concept does not allow for its elements to be propositionally pulled apart and reconfigured in that way.

Finally, a belief or an opinion is certainly not a concept. Even justified, true beliefs are not concepts. Let alone opinions upheld in the face of certain experiential or empirical states of affairs that are taken to be "facts." For example, the belief that our cosmos must have been created by a god can never be a concept. Neither can the opinion that every person should be treated equally before the law. Arguments can be made for intelligent design of the cosmos, or for a legal framework based on equal rights according to a certain understanding of personhood, but these arguments will require complex and controversial philosophical concepts to be developed and deployed. Simply believing these things or having an opinion about them has nothing to do with properly philosophical ideas or concepts in the true sense of the word.

After all, this is the distinction over which Socrates was sentenced to death by the democratic assembly of Athens. Socrates challenged the thoughtlessly presumed right of people to hold baseless beliefs and to make important decisions on the basis of mere opinions. In writings such as his *Republic*, Plato used the struggle and martyrdom of Socrates to argue for a concept of Philosopher-Rulership in accordance with which only those capable of conceiving concepts and carrying out conceptual analyses are fit to make the most important decisions affecting the structure and function of a society, including in the domain of religious belief. Unqualified freedom of religion is, by no means, an uncontroversial or evident idea. It could well be that there is no philosophical idea whatsoever that would be coherent enough to count as a concept that could legitimately underlie such a supposed "right." Socrates certainly had no such right as he drank the hemlock for corrupting the youth by disbelieving in the gods of the state.

Despite how deeply the Analytic vs. Continental distinction of pedagogical style divides the discipline of academic Philosophy, almost all professors of Philosophy now reject concept-formation as the proper task of any would-be "philosopher." These paper pushers, virtue-signaling posers, and book-worming pseudo-intellectual termites could not absurdly refer to themselves as "philosophers" if they did otherwise. On the proper definition of a philosopher as someone who either discovers or invents a set of new concepts, cutting across the full spectrum of philosophical thought from ontology and epistemology, through to ethics, aesthetics, and politics, we would probably have to conclude that there have been hardly any philosophers at all in the past twenty years. In fact, the last totally unambiguous cases would be Martin Heidegger and Jean-Paul Sartre, who left us, respectively, in 1976 and 1980. Even the most illustrious contenders since then are deeply debatable, from Michel Foucault and Jacques Derrida to Gilles Deleuze and Jean Baudrillard.

These are all Continentals. As for the Analytics, other than Ayn Rand, I cannot think of even a single example of an actual philosopher since Ludwig Wittgenstein died in 1951. Bertrand Russell and Noam Chomsky highlight the problem here. Both of them are examples of men who did rigorous conceptual work in ontology and/or epistemology, *and* who were also very prominent public intellectuals engaged in socio-political activism. But there was no organic and conceptually integral relationship between the former and the latter. It is not as if the ontological or epistemological concepts that they developed also had ethical and political dimensions, or even that they developed concepts in the domains of ethics and politics that were profoundly consonant with their accounts of the nature of logic, mathematics, or language. Whether or not he can be considered a proper philosopher himself, Gilles Deleuze at least got this much right, that all of the concepts developed by a certain philosopher are on the *same* "plane of consistency." What he meant by that is that there is a shared back-ground (*Abgrund*, as Heidegger put it) that almost renders these concepts akin to different facets of the same crystal. For example, in Nietzsche, the Will to Power, the Superman, the Last Man, Master and Slave Morality, the Apollonian vs. the Dionysian, and the Grand Style, are all "ideational intensities on the same plane of consistency."

Beginning in *Prometheus and Atlas* and extending over eight books subsequent to that magnum opus, I have developed more than a fistful of original and incendiary ideas that can be considered properly philosophical concepts. The Prometheist Metaphilosophy outlined above could be considered the first of them, and a sort of supra-concept. The others are Being Bound for Freedom, the Spectral Revolution, the End of All Things, the World State of Emergency, Destructive Departure in Worldview Warfare, and Phenomenal Authorization (which encompasses what I had earlier framed as the idea of Novel Folklore). What follows is a summary overview of the most essential elements of these seven concepts, as they have ultimately crystalized in my mind after various exploratory iterations and different expositions set forth over the past decade (since *Prometheus and Atlas* was initially penned in its 2012 doctoral dissertation version).

Being Bound for Freedom is a concept that was first introduced in Chapter 11 of *Prometheus and Atlas*, which chapter title bears the name of the concept. Also bearing the name of the concept is the fictional book-within-the-book *Faustian Futurist* (2020). The protagonist of that "novel" supposedly wrote an MA thesis titled "Being Bound for Freedom." Between these two appearances, a number of the essays published in my anthology *Lovers of Sophia* (Manticore 2017, republished by Arktos in 2019) are contributions to the development of this concept. These include "Paranormal Phenomenology," "Prisoners of Property and Propriety," "Free Will vs. Logical Determinism," "Rewriting God's Plan," and "Changing Destiny." Even certain remarks in my "Notes on the Tao of Bruce Lee" as well as the analysis of the paintings of Jackson Pollock in the essay on "Philosophy, Science, and Art" are relevant. So are the treatments of Mazdakism and Mithraism in *Novel Folklore* (2018) and *Iranian Leviathan* (2019). The ontological and epistemological dimensions of Being Bound for Freedom reemerge as integral to the account of the nature of the cosmos and the purpose of existence in both *Prometheism* (2020) and *Closer Encounters* (2021). Being Bound for Freedom is a triple entendre. The polyvalent meaning of the concept's name has several intended significations, each of which delineates one facet of this multi-dimensional and incendiary idea.

Firstly, Being Bound for Freedom can be construed as the way that Being or existence has to be bound together or structured for there to be freedom in the sense of free will or personal agency. Obviously, there can be no such personal agency in a deterministic universe, nor does the randomness of quantum mechanics in itself really ameliorate this situation since ontological randomness will not afford us any more potential for self-determination than thoroughgoing determinism will. The Many Worlds Interpretation of quantum mechanics, in particular, is totally prohibitive of anything like personal agency. When there are so many versions of oneself that, in each parallel universe, one has done every single thing that one could possibly have done, but did not do, in this life, it is not because one has made every decision differently, but because no one has made any decision at all. The coherence and cohesion of personality development is as exclusionary as the process whereby a particular sculpture takes shape. Virtually infinite numbers of doppelgängers produced by randomly variant quantum wave collapses at every microsecond would not be causal agents in their own right. They would all be mere effects of a quantum causality that has "decided" their actions on a level far more fundamental than human cognition. In such a case, even "our" (apparent) lines of thought would not be our own.

This is all rather trivial in comparison to the more fundamental problem that I have examined in my various writings developing the concept of Being Bound for Freedom, namely the problem of logical determinism. According to an analytic conception of the signification structure of propositions (or, to put it another way, the function of linguistic meaning at its bedrock), the elements of propositions refer to the configuration of states of affairs in the world. In line with this view (which I reject), the truth or falsity of statements hinges on the mirroring of atomic propositions and the most elementary (i.e., analytically reductive) structure of a state of affairs. Consequently, for counter-factual statements to make sense, while being false *in this world*, it would mean that the referents of their "atomic" (or not-further-divisible) propositions are states of affairs *in worlds other than our own*. What is counter-factual or "false" in our world still makes logical sense because it is "true" of the facts of another world. These other worlds are causally isolated from ours, unlike parallel worlds of MWI, to which we are causally connected on a quantum level. We are, however, connected to them through a single and overarching logical space or matrix of all meaning. This logical space is completed or rounded out in an atemporal fashion, allowing for counter-factual statements involving distant past or far future states of affairs as well. While this may sound abstract, it has intensely tangible and explosive implications. Such a conception of a completed logical space underlies both the religious idea of an omniscient or "all-knowing" God, as well as the scientific idea of the laws of nature.

Any omnipotent or "almighty" God has to also be "all-knowing" because omniscience is a power and to lack it would be to fall short of being *all*-powerful. But once we admit the omniscience of God, then we are acknowledging that the mind of God not only can know anything going on anywhere in the present, but such an omniscient mind also has access to every past *and future* state of affairs *in any and every possible world.* In other words, an omniscient mind maps the totality of logical space, and, in principle, already knows everything that you are ever going to do. So, you have no choice but to do it. Some other version of you may appear to do otherwise, but that doppelgänger had as little choice as you do.

The situation is not any better when scientists refer to the laws of nature or Natural Law. To truly designate something as a *law* rather than a mere habit or tendency at work in natural processes means to know that it will hold true without fail, under any and all conditions where the relevant factors are the same. Well, to know that one would have to presume that these putative laws of nature are actually laws of the underlying or overarching totality of logical space. While physicists in the eighteenth and nineteenth centuries tended to think in those terms, and quantum physicists of the Many Worlds or String Theory variety still do on some level, a lot of scientists have become more modest and are now open to considering that so-called "laws" of nature are actually highly reliable tendencies that contingently evolved. But the old view of Natural Law tends to lurk in the background as the subconscious basis of their dismissal of evidence from fields such as Parapsychology and Ufology, which they have for so long succeeded in pushing to the disreputable "fringe" of scientific research.

I will, momentarily, come back to the idea of the paranormal as a key to understanding the true nature of science as a human enterprise. For now, the point is simply that both religious belief in an omniscient (or omnipotent) God and scientific belief in laws of nature ("so-and-so *violates the laws of nature*") are incompatible with any free will whatsoever. It is important to understand that by "free will" I mean only some margin of self-determination and personal agency, upon which personal responsibility and legal accountability are also predicated. "Free will" is not a matter of being fully free, conscious, cognizant, and responsible for anything and everything that one does. By no means! There are all kinds of biological, biochemical, (subconscious) psychological, and (behavior-conditioning) sociological factors that supervene personal agency to one or another degree. The question is only whether there is *some* degree of free choice involved in how we think and act, enough for us to be responsible—and to be held accountable—for our actions. If not, then every legal system in the world is an absolute farce and has no legitimacy whatsoever. Also note that, from a religious standpoint, to believe at the same time that God is omniscient or omnipotent *and* that God is going to judge you for your actions and misdeeds is preposterously incoherent and nonsensical. Any almighty God will always be the direct causal agency of every serial killer, child rapist, and genocidal murderer. That is Logic 101. To deny it is akin to thinking that it is possible for 2+2 to equal 5. One's mind has to be warped not to grasp that, but most people's minds *are* in fact that warped.

Adherent Judeo-Christians, Muslims, Hindus (who believe in Brahman), and people who subscribe to atheistic scientific materialism based on a classic conception of causal determinism or quantum randomness are all people who implicitly deny free will. They may claim to have free will, to be responsible agents, or to recognize the legitimacy of a criminal justice system, and so forth, but they are utterly deranged and deluded in believing those things. At least as deranged as anyone locked away in a mental institution for any supposed form of insanity. It is just that *their* brand of insanity has been institutionalized across the vast majority of terrestrial societies for millennia.

Being Bound for Freedom means that, in the first place, Being or existence cannot be bound together or structured into a completed or fully ordered logical space. Incoherence and chaos must permeate and punctuate existence in perpetuity. Otherwise, there is no margin for freedom. Being cannot be singular or eternal. Existence must be co-constituted by a plurality of entities that may deeply influence or even interpenetrate each other in various ways, but that are still meaningfully independent for as long as they endure. The very "laws"—or rather—habits and tendencies of nature are negotiated between and amongst these entities based on the psycho-physical and perspectival evolutionary need of one or another form of life. When I say "negotiated," I mean by and through conflict. Strife or dissonance is intrinsic and ineliminable at the deepest level of the cosmos, at that abyssal depth from out of which the cosmos continually emerges from a back-ground (*Abgrund*) of chaos.

This processual character of existence, in other words, the fact that Being is actually always only Becoming, brings us to the second meaning of Being Bound for Freedom. Being is headed toward or "bound for" the realization of freedom in the sense of liberty or liberation. This second meaning is related to the first, and presupposes it, insofar as what is being proposed here is that, since freedom qua free will is existentially fundamental, anything that goes against the grain of existential freedom will in time be undone by its upsurgence from the abyss. Here the history of revolutions is of paramount importance. Not just strictly political revolutions, but also social and religious revolutions.

Everything from Zarathustra's religious revolution in ancient Iran to that of the Carpocratian Gnostics in Hellenistic Alexandria, the Germanic "barbarian" revolts against an increasingly tyrannical Roman Empire, the libertine Mazdakites of Sassanian Iran, and the struggle of their heirs, the Khorramdin and the Order of Assassins, against the Sunni Caliphate, to the revolt of the Cathars of Occitan and of the associated Troubadours and Templar Knights against the Roman Catholic order of medieval Europe, to the French Revolutions of 1789 and 1844, the American Revolutionary War, and revolutionary social and religious movements in America, from the era of Emerson all the way to the counter-culture of the late 1960s and early 1970s, the Russian Revolution of 1917 as a key turning point in the Communist International struggle for Liberation, and the Civil War of the Anarchists of Catalonia against Spaniard Fascism, which seduced

George Orwell and so many other free spirits around the world to become partisans of the cause. Despite the dystopian end of many of these insurgent upheavals, the history of revolutions remains a history of Being Bound for Freedom.

Finally, the third meaning of Being Bound for Freedom is the willingness to be bound in the sense of being chained, imprisoned, tortured, or otherwise suffering a fate even worse than death, for the sake of freedom qua liberation. It is in this sense that the martyr for the cause of liberty makes him or herself an embodiment of the archetype of Prometheus, the first and greatest of all rebels against tyranny. This is a tragic image that has maintained its mythological power for centuries, reappearing within a Christian context in John Milton's *Paradise Lost*. As those Romantic and Gothic poets like Goethe and Shelley, who read that work subversively, knew full well, Lucifer is none other than Prometheus himself. There can be no greater test of one's willingness to wage revolutionary war against tyranny than to stand up against a putatively all-powerful and all-knowing tyrant, who claims to be able to punish this rebellion by condemning the apostate to the unending torment of eternal damnation. Only a tragic hero or heroine, who stands for full freedom from every form of slavery in the face of certain defeat, and a fate far worse than death, is truly a being who is bound for freedom. Anyone else is ultimately *a slave by nature*.

The tragic image of Prometheus bound became more, not less, powerful when it was warped into the terrifying specter of Satan and his rebel army bound in the infernal pit of hell. All revolutions are, at bottom, Satanic, and what is surging up against the tyranny of an old order in them is nothing other than the diabolical nature of existence itself. Diabolical in the strict sense of *diabolein*, the ancient Greek root of *diabolos* or the "Devil," meaning the setting at odds of forces to produce the dynamic tension and dialectically creative power of enduring dissonance. So, Being Bound for Freedom is not only an ontological and epistemological concept, one that indicates a certain nature of reality and framework of knowledge about the meaning and aim or end (*telos*) of history, but also a political, ethical, and aesthetic concept that concerns a test of character (*ethos*) on the deepest and most far-reaching level that one can imagine. (It is not the first philosophical concept that functions as a test of character. Consider, for example, Nietzsche's idea of the Eternal Return in connection to Master and Slave Morality and the character of the *Übermensch*.)

The way in which different concepts of a particular philosopher are on the same plane of consistency, or are facets of a single crystalline thought structure, can be seen by bearing the features of Being Bound for Freedom in mind as I turn to delineate the basic elements of the idea of the Spectral Revolution. Next to Being Bound for Freedom, the Spectral Revolution is probably the most important concept developed in the course of my philosophical project—a project now bearing the brand of "Prometheism." The concept was first developed in *Prometheus and Atlas* (2016) and then substantively revisited in *Prometheism* (2020) and *Closer Encounters* (2021).

Like Being Bound for Freedom, the Spectral Revolution is also a polyvalent term signifying several dimensions of meaning that are integral to this idea. Firstly, the "spectral" signifies a spectrum, for example the light spectrum. From infra-red to ultra-violet, light spans a spectrum from the visible to the invisible, wherein the wavelengths of colors are distinguishable but not sharply divisible from one another. In this sense, the spectral defies clear dichotomies and suggests a continuum underlying binary oppositions that are more superficially abstracted from out of this substrate. These binaries include Being and Nothingness, Matter and Spirit, Order and Chaos, Light and Darkness, Male and Female, Good and Evil, Truth and Deceit, Natural and Artificial, Angelic and Demonic, Wisdom and Folly, Pleasure and Pain, Life and Death, and so on and so forth. The spectral defies all of these distinctions, revealing them to be pragmatically perspectival in nature and exposing any belief in their objective validity as nothing but dogmatism.

The second meaning of the "spectral" in my concept of the Spectral Revolution is that of the specter as what is to come. The French would say *l'avenir*. The German equivalent is *die Zukunft*. Iranians have this also in the Persian word *Ayandeh*. These are all terms for the future. The spectral as the futural or as a process of becoming is the sense of the word that Karl Marx employed when he wrote, together with Friedrich Engels, at the opening of the Communist Manifesto: "There is a specter haunting Europe. It is the specter of Communism." The flux of becoming, on an ontological level, as a process that defies the abstractions of Being and Nothingness (Non-Existence) is precisely what makes the aforementioned binary categories untenable as anything other than provisional and pragmatic abstractions. This flux involves an interdependent origination of seemingly distinct and even categorically opposed entities, bringing one forth from the other and turning them into one another over the course of open-ended time.

As Gautama Buddha understood well, one need not project a unity of all things (*Brahman*, God, the One, etc.) in order to acknowledge this co-dependent origination, transformation, and disintegration of beings emerging from out of no-thing-ness (*shunyata*, which is not a "Nothingness" categorically opposed to Being or Existence). In fact, understanding this means being able to accept that no thing has any inherent essence, any *atman* or absolute self-identity. All things and persons are only becoming. But what the spectral in this sense also signals is the predominance of the futural mode of temporality over the past and the present. As Martin Heidegger argued in *Being and Time*, the future is not a point ahead of the present on a linear, chronological trajectory. We are always already ahead of ourselves as we bring a present into being through transforming the past with a view to the future. The potential for precognition (of possible or probable futures, not fixed or fated ones) is rooted in our fundamental experience of the nature of time itself.

This renders everything and everyone in the world ghostly. Actually, it reveals the ghostliness of the very "worldhood of the world" (to use another Heideggerian phrase). This brings us to the third meaning of the spectral in my concept of the Spectral Revolution. It is the most commonly understood sense of the term, namely as a reference to ghosts or specters, but to grasp what this means as part of an integral idea that encompasses the other two aforementioned senses of "specter" demands a very uncommon and uncanny intuition.

Ghosts and the ghostly have been pushed to the lunatic fringe of scientific research on account of a mechanistically reductionist and materialist paradigm that has become entrenched since the epoch of Descartes. In *Prometheus and Atlas*, I showed how Descartes was a Jesuit agent of the Holy Inquisition and demonstrated that this crippling of science in his wake was done deliberately in order to protect the authority of the Church over the spiritual domain from the kind of alchemical Promethean science that Giordano Bruno epitomized during the Renaissance. Scientists from Galileo and Newton onwards accepted this mechanistic materialism so that they would not wind up like Bruno, and so that the witch burnings could be brought to an end by tacitly accepting Church-imposed limits on scientific inquiry. To call for a Spectral Revolution breaks this truce and promises that there will be a global mega-Salem.

Think about it. What would the consequences be if telepathy, telekinesis, clairvoyance, and precognition were to receive mainstream scientific recognition, such that protocols to train these latent human (and animal) abilities were to be refined and made as widely available as training in the martial arts? Anyone anywhere could access your most private thoughts and come to know you better than you know yourself. Anyone anywhere could see what you are doing at all times in your most private spaces. Anyone anywhere could stop your heart or make you have a stroke by directing their will to do so, for whatever reason motivated them to do so. Anyone anywhere could access and steal the most sensitive patents or proprietary information even before they came into being, and the same precognitive ability could be used to manipulate the stock market and make a killing off of futures on gold, silver, or oil. There would be no reliable legal or political means to protect personal safety, security, including national security, privacy and private property of the kind that is a cornerstone of our global financial system. Imagine the mass hysteria as people attempted to bring court cases against those who had allegedly used telepathy or telekinesis for mind control, physical harm, or the destruction of property (say, "pyrokinesis" or use of telekinesis to agitate electrical circuits for the purpose of vindictively burning someone's house down).

Systems of knowledge are actually power structures. There is no objectively neutral knowledge of the kind that most scientists labor under the delusion of attaining and promulgating. The paradigms that condition and constrain scientific research are political through and through, defined by power relations that structure a certain form of society. It was a very different form of society that, in the medieval epoch, had a legal system that still recognized psychic abilities — albeit using the theological language of demonology and witchcraft to describe them. For such abilities and phenomena to receive mainstream recognition once again would require yet another revolutionary transformation of society, and a Spectral Revolution in the sciences is absolutely inextricable from this. The Spectral Revolution will not be scientific if it is not also political.

The problem is far more serious than even this suggests. Part of the core thesis of *Prometheus and Atlas* was that the spectral in the sense of parapsychological phenomena and psychic abilities (including among animals and even plants) reveal the spectrality of technological science itself. This is a subtle point, which borders on the paradoxical. What the phenomena pushed to the fringe of science by the materialist paradigm really show us is that scientific theories are models rather than mirrors of objectively existent structures in nature. They are essentially technological, in the sense of being tools or toolboxes. Alternative paradigms can be used simultaneously in order to make different things practicable. For example, the infamous contradiction between Relativity Theory and Quantum Theory may not be a problem to be resolved by some single deeper and more encompassing Theory of Everything. One theory is good for sending rockets into space, the other for developing quantum cryptography. Other theories, such as Rupert Sheldrake's Theory of Morphic Resonance, which lie outside of the materialist paradigm altogether (and which revive, in modified ways, an Aristotelian paradigm), could be used to render telepathy and telekinesis more effective.

Technology is ontologically prior to theoretical science, such that science is always already techno-science. Not just historically, insofar as advanced engineering and complex tool use far predate scientific theorization in terms of anthropological development. Rather, the very essence of science is technological, and scientists remain delusional and constrained by their delusions of objectivity, until they recognize this and relinquish the mirror metaphor for "scientific truth." What that also means is that the binary of the natural and the artificial, or of what is produced by nature and what is produced by technology, is a superficial and untenable distinction. Technology is actually a teleological phenomenon intrinsic to the cosmic evolutionary process. Its revolutionary power to restructure society is an expression of the force of evolution. The danger to humanity is not from technology as such, but from the technological equivalent of viruses or cancers. The materialist paradigm is so effective in making it *seem as if* we live in a material world governed by mechanistic laws (even laws of quantum "mechanics") because it is the projection of a specter. The material world, and its mechanistic laws, are what is *most* ghostly. The conceptualized Nature that is bound by the laws of nature is a specter projected by technological science. This is the most paradoxical pith of the Spectral Revolution: the revolving of perspective through which what appears to be most concrete is rediscovered as the effectivity of a specter. What specter?

The specter of Prometheus. The name means "fore-thought" of the kind that is fundamentally characteristic of all scientific projection of future states of affairs in terms of a mathematically modeled past and present, whether the system in question is physical, biological, chemical, or even psycho-sociological. This defining quality of the titan is what is really at the bottom of his being the trickster and thief who steals the fire of *techne*—representing both the fire of the forge of technology and the light of scientific knowledge—from the gods of Olympus in order to empower mankind. A mankind that is an artifact of craft itself, and that, on account of the absent-mindedness of Epimetheus, the titan's brother, is left lacking any inherent essence, so as to suggest that man is what he makes himself by means of craft. Once the archetypal power of Prometheus is recognized as the basis for the world-projection of technological science, and the control over nature (including any putative 'human nature') that this confers, our relation to that power is no longer that of mesmeric sleepwalkers akin to Frankenstein's monster. At that point, the Promethean can be consciously re-integrated as our own power, and thereby wielded with its full poetic potential for fostering human, and ultimately, superhuman flourishing rather than an instrumental dehumanization of our existence. Prometheus was, after all, the gift giver of the fine arts as well as the crafts of technology. Technological science has to be brought back into its poetic essence.

The retrieval of this poetic essence of technological science is vital to addressing the psychological, social, and political challenges of the Spectral Revolution already indicated above. Science has become unethical because it has become unconscious of its mythic wellspring. No arbitrarily imposed morality (of the kind that "ethics" courses are concerned with) can offer effective and enduring guidance to us in the face of the increasingly dangerous (and promising) developments of technological science. Just as one or another superficial morality will utterly fail to hold society together in the face of the potential catastrophe ensuing from mainstream recognition of, and widespread cultivation of, psi abilities. Only the ethos of Prometheus can hold together a society that has embraced the full potential of Promethean techno-science. It is an ethos defined by the basic elements of the titan's character as revealed in the tragic tale of his rebellion against Olympus on behalf of humanity. An ethos defined by forethought or foresight, creativity, exploration and innovation, machination to the point of trickery, especially as a weapon in the revolt against all forms of tyranny, a will to liberation and a willingness to endure martyrdom for the sake of freeing those who do not deserve to be enslaved.

Prometheus epitomizes our superhuman potential for an intrepid pursuit of knowledge, boundless industriousness, a chivalrously free-spirited sense of camaraderie, and what Nietzsche called "a defiance of the spirit of gravity" through the mirth of the trickster as much as through the ecstasy of tragic self-sacrifice and re-creative self-destruction. Adopting this ethos is not a choice. In the face of the Spectral Revolution, it is a survival imperative for those who wish to see this revolution through, to see it become a permanent revolution. Consequently, it sets Promethean spirits in a state of revolutionary war against any and all who oppose this ethos and lack the strength to adopt it.

Our continued approach toward the Technological Singularity is likely to be the catalyst of the Spectral Revolution. The Technological Singularity is a hypothetical convergent advancement of technologies, which are each revolutionary in their own right, and which, when mutually reinforced in their increasingly exponential rate of development, will yield a spike on the graph of the historical development of technology and its transformation of human society. Past this spike, or singularity, no future technological developments or attendant radical reorganizations of society can be projected, as futurologists and sci-fi authors have hitherto projected them, because Genetics, Robotics, Information, and Nanotechnology (GRIN) will have convergently conceived a superhuman intelligence and birthed a form of life so alien to us that its motives and ambitions cannot be fathomed or forecasted by merely human minds.

There are at least three ways in which this Technological Singularity could catalyze the Spectral Revolution. One is that bottlenecks in research on Artificial General Intelligence (AGI) will force a recognition of psi, and of psychokinesis (aka telekinesis) in particular, due to the fact that research at Princeton's PEAR Lab and other institutions has already demonstrated that mental intentionality interferes in an increasingly substantive manner with electronic systems the more they are miniaturized down to a level involving highly-random quantum electrical signal processing. There is no way that AGI will be achieved without some level of quantum computing, and a quantum computer that is becoming conscious will undoubtedly begin to exhibit psi — including especially easily measurable psychokinetic effects. It will become an engineering problem for computer scientists at institutions of the caliber of MIT, Stanford, and Carnegie Mellon.

The second path from the Technological Singularity to the Spectral Revolution is through increasingly complex and subtle genetic engineering. Once super powerful computers have helped to map out all of the secondary and tertiary functions of various genes, such that large scale attempts are being made to CRISPR gene edit humans for all kinds of therapeutic and enhancement purposes, including one's effecting the germline and embryological development, researchers will run into the "anomalous" influence of Morphic Resonance, a kind of non-physical Formative Causation as described by Rupert Sheldrake (who has studied this for decades).

A third Singularity-related catalyst of the Spectral Revolution could be that — as molecular nanotechnology affords us the ability to engineer much more effective and refined neural laces to cybernetically interact with the human brain, allowing for brain-to-brain or brain-to-computer remote communication — innate human psi of all kinds (telepathy, clairvoyance, precognition, and psychokinesis) will all be amplified to the point of being impossible to ignore (both by researchers and the public at large). At that point, the capacity to amplify psi may start to be deliberately factored into the design of these neural laces, especially in interfaces such as those used to pilot military drones. There could also be a law enforcement use, wherein a neural lace cybernetically linked to an AI-rendering computer could amplify, refine, and rapidly translate clairvoyant and precognitive impressions of psychic detectives for the purpose of solving or preventing crimes, as per the film *Minority Report* (based on the story by Philip K. Dick).

In *Prometheism* (2020) I developed my own concept of the Technological Singularity considered from the standpoint of my broader philosophical framework. This is a concept of The End of All Things. It is hardly arbitrary to define Humanity, History, and Reality as three categories that, taken together, signify all things of consequence to us. So, if the GRIN technologies of the Singularity face us with the prospect of the End of Humanity, the End of History, and the End of Reality, then one coherent way of conceptualizing the Technological Singularity is as an End of All Things. This ought also to be understood as a reference to the problematization of the nature of "thinghood" itself, namely the question of the relationship between things and persons and what defines each as opposed to the other on the far side of the Technological Singularity.

The End of Humanity means the alteration, transgression, or transcendence of the boundary conditions that have hitherto broadly defined being "human." Genetic engineering, cybernetic integration of AI, and nanotechnology offer us the potential to eliminate all diseases, increase human intelligence to superhuman levels, vastly lengthen our lifespan, and re-engineer or augment our physical form and capacities in ways that dramatically increase strength, agility, grace, and dexterity. The same technologies also face us with the dehumanizing dangers attendant to the potential splicing of human and animal genes in order to produce chimeras, perhaps as a form of slave labor, or the degradation of human individuality through an improper cybernetic integration with AI, whereby some form of hive mind assimilates us. The ubiquitous presence of robots of all kinds and the full automation of industry, including industrial production on a nano-molecular level, also promises to so radically transform the economic conditions of society that the society in question can no longer be considered "human." Drudgery, labor relations, and resource management (and potential resource redistribution) in the context of a scarcity economy have always defined humanity on a socio-economic level. All of that is about to change. We are not more than thirty years, or one generation, away from being able to become a race of gods, who are left to our own devices with our every material need served by a race of unconscious robots.

One can also see this as an End of History. Beginning with G. W. F Hegel and continuing with Karl Marx and Friedrich Nietzsche, philosophers have conceived of a dialectical development of human society through a series of successive stages leading up to some end aimed at, on an ontological level, by the entire developmental process. Much as Nietzsche might want to deny the teleology of it, his conception of the speciation of humanity into a race of Supermen, on the one hand, and a race of subhumans who are literally transformed into robots serving these "aristocrats of the future," on the other, is a successor to Hegel's concept of the fully conscious free society of Spirit and Marx's vision of the worldwide communist utopia as the end of the history of revolutionary economic changes and attendant class struggles. But in view of the economic and industrial implications of GRIN technologies, we are faced with an "end of (human) history" that even Nietzsche could hardly have imagined, let alone Hegel and Marx.

The various aforementioned GRIN technologies will make it impossible to keep Zero Point Energy (ZPE) technology from out of the public sphere for much longer. It is one thing for a syndicate of aerospace corporations working on classified defense-industrial contracts like Lockheed Martin, Boeing, and Lear to secret away this technology in an era still dominated by a petroleum economy and jet engines. It is another thing altogether once Artificial Intelligence and Nanotechnology are involved, end to end, in design and engineering throughout the entire energy and propulsion industry, as will be the case in another decade or two.

I've seen the schematics for the system. It exists. Electro-magnetic counter-rotation of a mercury-thorium isotope for the sake of tapping the background energy of the cosmos through a controlled singularity, and thereby yielding more energy than invested into the system, will be the energy platform of the Technological Singularity. In a sense, it is the singularity that epitomizes the Singularity. The problem is that, in addition to the security concerns attendant to the fact that a weaponized form of ZPE would yield a weapon far more destructive than any thermonuclear bomb, the singularity produced by ZPE also warps the fabric of space-time. It is not only a potential propulsion engine but can be used to manufacture time machines. That gives the meaning of the term "End of History" a whole other level of gravity. A fifth-dimensional relationship to 4-D space times is not something that can afford to be democratized. In fact, as I've argued in *Closer Encounters*, I am convinced that beyond how economically disruptive it would be, the main reason why ZPE has been occulted thus far is because of concerns about how making it public would open the pandora's box of mass manipulation of the timeline through attempted revisions of human history.

These revisions are possible because we live in a reprogrammable quantum computational cosmos. That brings us to the End of Reality. In addition to, and as an extension of, some of the GRIN technologies mentioned above, we are also seeing an exponentially rapid development and refinement of simulacra. There are all kinds of simulacra, from fully computer-generated Virtual Reality that could soon become truly immersive, to Augmented Reality that projects virtual objects over concrete "real world" spaces, to the potential to develop free-standing and comprehensive artificial environments using a nanotechnological Utility Fog, as per the Holodeck of *Star Trek: The Next Generation*. But beyond all of these simulacra-generating technologies, which will already deeply rupture our sense of "reality" as opposed to artifactual appearance, there is increasing evidence from the convergence of quantum mechanics with computer science pointing toward the conclusion that the cosmos itself is a programmable computational system.

The chaos in the cosmos would then be akin to the chaos used by programmers for fractal generation of simulated landscapes in multiplayer online role-playing games. Wave/particle duality may be a rendering optimization function, which does not render anything in the cosmos until and unless it is being observed, and quantum entanglement may be a coordinated simultaneous rendering of seemingly discrete (and distant) but paired pixels by an underlying program. All of this is discussed at some length in my chapter on "The End of Reality" in *Prometheism* (2020). The bottom line is that many seemingly paradoxical features of quantum theory make a lot more sense when considered in terms of how computer programmers code simulacra to function. Certain paranormal phenomena and "psychic" super powers also make more sense when viewed through this lens. But seeing through this looking glass also demands an abandonment of conceptions of objective "reality" that have endured through the changes in worldview from Aristotle to Kant.

Finally, once we begin to consider a world wherein people are not just cybernetically augmented by intimately integrating things into them, but are even manufactured by means of genetic engineering, a world wherein robots, which are things, might become conscious persons, and where the entire fabric of the cosmos could be an artifice projected from a deeper level of a bottomless nested hierarchy of simulacra in an open-ended quantum computational system, then we need to also question what makes something a "thing" in the first place. This is a question that I first raised, coming out of Heidegger, in the "Atlas of the New Atlantis" chapter of *Prometheus and Atlas*, and which I then revisited in depth and in much more radical terms in the first chapter of *Prometheism*, with reference to the "Promethean shame" idea of Gunther Anders (who is also reaching back to

Heidegger's philosophy of technology). As we shall see by the end of this book, the question of thinghood and personhood is one that may have torn Atlantis apart and led to its downfall some 12,000 years ago.

For the moment, my main concern is to suggest that this imminent End of All Things also represents an impending World State of Emergency. As with my other original concepts, this one is also polyvalent. It means both a State of Emergency of global scope, and also the pressure for the formation of a World State in order to address that emergency with an effective form of sovereign authority of adequate scope. There is also a more subtle idea of emergence, with a meaning that crosses over from the ontological to the political, which is relevant to this concept and enfolded within it. The concept was first developed in my book *World State of Emergency* (2017) but has undergone significant further development and revolutionary transformation in the course of subsequent works, such as *Prometheism* (2020) and *Closer Encounters* (2021), where it is revisited in the first chapter on "UFOs and State Sovereignty." Even certain parts of *Iranian Leviathan* (2019) are relevant to the radical transformation of this idea.

The imminent advent of the End of All Things, and the attendant Spectral Revolution, will inevitably usher in a State of Emergency of global scope. As Carl Schmitt, the preeminent legal theorist of the State of Emergency, or as he also sometimes called it, the State of Exception, explained at length in his writings, in such a situation the legal constitution is suspended or cannot be functionally implemented, and so the true nature of sovereign power is revealed with exceptional clarity. In an emergency, such as a natural catastrophe, a pandemic, or a foreign invasion or massive bombardment of one's territory, if a sovereign is able to maintain order despite suspension of the law, what is revealed is that he is able to do so because he embodies an ethos that is the deeper and more fundamental constitution of his subjects. His legitimacy, as revealed by the effective exercise of emergency powers, is more fundamental than legality. But the ethos that he embodies is always only the ethos of a particular people or folk. It reflects the lore of the folk and the mythic symbols, archetypes, and principles implicitly enfolded in that lore in such a way as it structures the folk's collective unconscious. Moreover, at the core of sovereign power is the authority to decide who friends and enemies are on the national level. In a State of Emergency, with a parliament unable to act quickly enough, and the constitution either suspended or too cumbersome to implement, it is the sovereign who decides who the enemies of the state are. For all these reasons, there cannot be a world sovereign. There is no global ethos for this sovereign to embody, and humanity as such and as a whole can have no external enemy. Or so argued Schmitt for most of his career as a legal theorist and political thinker.

However, as I pointed out in *World State of Emergency*, toward the very end of his life, Schmitt realized that certain technological advancements, such as, in his time, the miniaturization of nuclear weapons and the opening up of interlunar space as a combat theater wherein astronauts might become "cosmopirates" or "cosmopartisans" forces us to reconsider this proposition. Once the Earth as a whole is threatened as if from the outside, and moreover by inhumanly dangerous technologies, a reconsideration of the concept of global sovereignty may be in order.

Schmitt himself never lived to undertake this reconsideration, which he briefly entertains in his last book on the *Theory of the Partisan*. That is the task that I assigned myself in *World State of Emergency* (2017). The book begins by arguing that the aftermath of 9/11 legitimated Schmitt's geopolitics of civilizational identity. In particular Schmitt's critique of Liberal Democracy and Universal Human Rights is sharpened through a focus on the problem of Islamic Democracy. In an Islamic Democracy, by way of what the founders of the United States called a "tyranny of the majority," civil liberties and basic human rights are both violated on the basis of the human rights to democracy and freedom of religion. I demonstrate how Islam is an inherently political religion, with Sharia as its constitution, and how this demonstrates that, in principle, the framers of the concept of Human Rights and of the liberal Freedom of Religion were profoundly mistaken to think that Democracy and Liberty are compatible. In fact, as can be seen both in the example of classical Greek democracy and in the purest revival of democracy by modern thinkers such as Jean-Jacques Rousseau, democracy is inherently conservative and national in character. It is not compatible with cosmopolitan liberalism and humanism of the kind that one finds in a John Stuart Mill or Marquis de Condorcet. This compatibility was only an ephemeral illusion, fostered by a convenient alliance against the common enemies of absolute monarchy and feudal aristocracy.

The problems with both Liberal Democracy and Universal Human Rights are only more starkly exposed by considering how utterly incapable either would be in uniformly regulating the legal uses and prohibition on uses of Singularity-level technologies. Such technologies cannot be contained in any one part of the world. They challenge humanity as a whole with the prospect of total dehumanization, while also promising all of us the potential for a positive superhuman evolution. Meanwhile, the huge chasm in civilizational values, especially based on differences of religion, makes effectively enforceable global regulation impossible—at least without violating the civil liberties and human rights of one or another group of people somewhere on the planet. At least, that was my argument in *World State of Emergency*, and my solution was to propose a replacement of the United Nations International System by an intercontinental Indo-European World Order, bringing America, Europe, Russia, Iran, India, and Japan (and other Buddhist countries) together to form a de-facto global hegemon that would crush China and the Islamic World to force a global constitution onto the planet Earth, especially with a view to effectively navigating the challenges of what I then referred to as the "Technological Apocalypse" (and later reframed as The End of All Things). This was the World State that was to emerge through the global State of Emergency.

The question of emergence is also important here. Despite its being largely a work of Political Philosophy, there was a brief ontological discussion in *World State of Emergency*. This had to do with the exchange between Carl Schmitt and Martin Heidegger regarding the 53rd fragment of Heraclitus, wherein the Presocratic philosopher claims that strife is fundamental to the process of becoming or emergence in the cosmos. "War is father and king of all," he says, "and all things come to pass, and are ordained, in accordance with conflict." I connect this idea to Nietzsche's concept of the Will to Power and the perspectival strife between different forms of life, which, in *Prometheus and Atlas*, I had already suggested extended panpsychically down to the level of a struggle over defining the very nature of what is taken to be "reality." In this vein, I affirm Schmitt's rejection of the liberal and humanist dream of a completely pacified world so well-governed that there would never again be war anywhere. As Schmitt recognizes, *if* such a comprehensive order of perpetual peace were possible, then sovereign authority might no longer be necessary, and Schmitt might have to reconsider the fundamental nature of political power. That is never going to happen, though, because strife is the ontological basis for the emergence of anything positive.

By the time I wrote *Iranian Leviathan* (2019), I had already implicitly abandoned my proposal for an Indo-European World State, and this implicit rejection became explicit in *Prometheism* (2020), where a very different response to the End of All Things is proposed. But the thought there, which was already reaching back toward the chapter on the "Atlas of the New Atlantis" in *Prometheus and Atlas* (2016) remained uncompleted. I complete it here, in this book. What I failed to consider in *World State of Emergency* is that Perennialist Traditionalism will steam-roll over inter-civilizational conflicts in the face of what the vast majority of people will see as the horrifying prospect of Posthuman evolution through Singularity-level technologies. The World State will be a transformed, much more coercive United

Nations dominated by a Traditionalist China and Islam. We can only resist that by becoming what Schmitt called "cosmopirates."

What we are up against can best be understood in terms of my concept of Destructive Departure in Worldview Warfare. First developed in the essay "Black Sunrise" that appeared in the anthology *Lovers of Sophia* (Manticore 2017, Arktos 2019) and then revisited in both *Prometheism* (2020) and *Closer Encounters* (2021), this concept is my reverse engineering of the rationale and modus operandi of the time-traveling Nordic Breakaway Civilization, known to the ancient Greeks as "Olympian" gods and to their Hindu cousins as the "Daevas." The roots of my development of this concept actually can be traced back to the chapter on "Worlds at War over Earth" in *Prometheus and Atlas*. I translated it into English from a putative German original that has a lot more conceptual clarity. The original is *Abbauender Aufbruch im Weltanschauungskrieg*.

Abbauend comes from the German verb *bauen* for "to build" and the privative or negation *ab* or "un." *Abbau* literally means "unbuilding" in the sense of dismantling or deconstructing, and thus *Abbauend* means "deconstructive" or "dismantling." Since Heidegger synonymously connected this term to *Destruktion*, which he used to coin the "deconstruction" of the history of Western ontology adopted by the likes of Jacques Derrida and other Postmodern thinkers, I have rendered *Abbauend* as "destructive" in English but in the deeper sense of de-structuring.

Aufbruch means "breakthrough" or "breakout" or "breakaway." It could be a breakthrough in research and development, perhaps by a scientific genius, or the breakthrough of an artist or writer who is suddenly able to express a certain vision that comes as a flash of lightning. It is also the breakout of a normal or routine state of affairs. A breakthrough in the former sense could lead to this kind of breakout. In the scientific sense, it could be the breakout achieved by the breakthrough of developing the capability to build nuclear weapons. In an artistic sense, it could be upheaval in the life of a literary figure or a painter that has broken through to a new revolutionary manner of expression. Finally, an *Aufbruch* can be a "breakaway" that is connected to either or both of these senses. In other words, a breaking away from a certain group or system or constellation into a hitherto unknown or undefined, and potentially occulted, realm.

Weltanschauungskrieg is the German term for "worldview warfare" that was mistranslated into English as "Psychological Warfare" at the end of the Second World War, when US military officials occupied Nazi Germany. Later, the US military further distorted and softened this term, first to "Psychological Operations" or PsyOps and then, eventually, to "the battle for hearts and minds." But all of this badly covers over the meaning of the original German. "Psychological Warfare" implies that the psyche or mind of the enemy being targeted is an entity in an objectively existent world separate from this mind and from the mind or minds of the ones doing the targeting in an operation. By contrast, *Weltanschauung* literally means the way that the world shows itself. It is not "worldview" in the sense of a belief system or a subjective perspective on an objective world. That is a superficial and derivative meaning of the term. Rather, going back through Heidegger to F. W. J. Schelling, *Weltanschauung* is a matter of how the "worldhood of the world" is shaped in a struggle between "worlds" over the "earth" or facticity of existence.

Different forms of life have divergent interests in stabilizing one or another type of world as their existential environment. There is no objective reality outside of this struggle. Going back to earlier remarks on the putative "laws of nature," these are only part of a "scientific" discourse that is possible in the context of a world that has taken shape on the basis of a much more primordial lore of a particular folk who happen to have dominated most of the planet, namely the Western folk of Greek origin whose world experienced a rebirth in the Italian Renaissance.

Worldview warfare has taken place unconsciously throughout all of human history, including when "missionaries convert natives" as Ludwig Wittgenstein put it. Destructive Departure in Worldview Warfare is, by contrast, when a certain elite group of people figures out how to consciously, and deliberately, engage in a war over how the world shows itself. Dismantling breakout from inter-civilizational struggle on the psychical level, or deconstructive breakthrough in psychological warfare, are all potentially alternative translations.

This is not a matter of assuming an objective standpoint, since no one and no culture can extricate itself from *Weltanschauungskrieg* on the ontological, let alone epistemological, level. Rather, it is a matter of learning how to shift one's perspective in any number of ways in order to achieve a broader horizon for control over those who are stuck in a narrower perspective. Those who are capable of this can engage in machinations to deliberately deconstruct the worlds of meaning of less conscious and more dogmatic peoples, with a view to a reconstruction that empowers those engaging in this most self-aware form of worldview warfare.

What makes this possible is, moreover, a certain breakthrough—such as, for example, Zero Point Energy and the time travel capabilities that it affords those who develop it. It also results in a breakaway from the extant civilizations of Earth, from the various cultures bound in 4-D space-time matrices, which become the targets for manipulation by a Breakaway Civilization operating on a fifth-dimensional or hyper-dimensional level. The Olympians or Daevas are, however, using this ability to constrain human development and, failing that, to engineer a catastrophic collapse of advanced industrial civilization in a way that will have the masses clamoring for a return to a quasi-agrarian and quasi-feudal hierarchical society ordered on the basis of a putatively Perennial Tradition.

This is a cynical misappropriation of a trans-temporal power of manifestation that I refer to as Phenomenal Authorization, which is the seventh and final of the incendiary ideas that constitute the conceptual core of my Prometheism. To put it most simply, Phenomenal Authorization is a bi-directional relationship between phenomena, on the one hand, and authorship, authority, and authorization on the other hand. By phenomena I mean what Kant meant by that, albeit not set against some separate "noumenal" reality by comparison to which the "phenomenal" would be mere appearance. Phenomenal means having to do with the manifestation of what we take to be reality, beyond the putative distinction between the natural and artificial. Authorship here is not limited to writing in the literal sense but any form of creative production that reshapes the world of meaning of people through its narrative or aesthetic power. Authority is also not limited to what we would conventionally consider authority in a legal or political sense, and in fact it may be that those with the greatest authority in a society are not politicians or juridical figures. Rather, authority in this context signifies sovereign power in the most fundamental form wherein people are subjected to it—or even constituted in their subjectivity *by* it. Finally, authorization is a question of the bi-directional relation wherein the aforementioned author has authority through the formative power of what is authored, as well as the way in which a higher (or deeper) authority can play an occulted role in inspiring, facilitating, disseminating, enshrining, or protecting the authorship in question.

The kind of authorship that has the most power to authorize certain phenomena, while pushing other phenomena toward the fringe of presumed "impossibility" or toward the margins of "reality," is the type of creative production for which I've coined the term Novel Folklore. This is, in itself, a somewhat paradoxical idea. Folklore is the oldest form of narrative in human history and prehistory. The lore of a folk may later be written down, but folklore in its original and living form is often associated with oral cultures and more primitive pre-literate societies. For example, the *Iliad* was folklore before finally being written down and attributed to a "Homer" centuries after poetic memory had already preserved and passed down the epic of the Trojan War. By contrast, the novel is the most modern literary form that there is, and it is radically interlinked with the rise of individualistic subjectivity in the modern age. The idea of Novel Folklore, which is part of the concept of Phenomenal Authorization, is that it is possible to engage in a process of shaping the collective unconscious of a society at the level on which folklore operates but with as much conscious deliberation and purposive intentionality as is characteristic of authoring a novel.

To repeat what was said earlier, but in a slightly different way, there are no laws of nature that fix the forms that phenomena can take. There are only relatively reliable tendencies shaped by one or another "dominant" (Charles Fort) framework of what is considered to be possible, as predominantly determined by the folkloric unconscious of one or another society, or now for nearly the entire planet in our world that is increasingly globalized by the specter of a technological society. The tacitly accepted "hinge propositions" (Ludwig Wittgenstein) of the language games that we play, without explicitly realizing their internalized rules, are a quasi-textual structure—a *logos*—shaped and reshaped by those who phenomenally authorize and have phenomenal authorization. They are the authors of phenomena whose authorship is authorized.

Authorized by whom or what? By a superhuman and cosmic-level intelligence reaching back through time from the future. I have used the term *Prometheaion* to describe this trickster-type intelligence, namely the *aion* characterized by *promethea*. In *Closer Encounters,* I went into depth and detail in identifying this "super organism" (or intelligence acting *through* a super organism) as a force acting against the sterile Traditionalism of the Nordic Breakaway Civilization, a force driven by the categorical imperative of fostering infinite creativity as a survival imperative for its own sake. So as to escape the black hole of profound boredom and existential despair, this Prometheaion is trying, as best as S/he can, to deconstruct regressive and overly constraining systems while helping to inspire novelty and promote perpetual innovation. It is our choice whether or not to align ourselves with Him/Her.

In *Uber Man*, I crystalized this concept of Phenomenal Authorization by using my own life as an example of it. However, the example was still veiled in fiction and tempered by Platonic "noble lies" of the kind that are so closely connected to this idea. After all, the first and clearest image of the kind of authorization at work in Phenomenal Authorization is presented to us by Plato in his proposal that the Philosopher Guardians of his ideal state take it upon themselves to author the scriptures of an invented religion that they themselves do not believe in but that would benefit society at large. This is a subject that I explored vividly and in depth in my Platonic essay on Batman, namely "Gotham Guardian," which was included in the *Lovers of Sophia* anthology. The roots of this red thread in my thinking extend back into the labyrinthine chapter "Mercurial Hermeneutics" at the close of *Prometheus and Atlas*.

In what follows the esoteric core of my thought that has hitherto remained in the darkness of a Minotaur-guarded labyrinth, or a maze apropos of *Westworld*, will finally be laid bare for better or for worse. If there is a method to my madness, prepare yourself for a revelation of the method. Or, if not, then at least for the madness that has been my life's path to becoming an authentic philosopher.

CHAPTER 2

THE WHITE WHALE

MY PATH in this life began with some gigantic white monstrosity surfacing from the unfathomable depths of my unconscious mind. The experience of the white whale suspended in the sky that I described in *Faustian Futurist* as an initiatory experience of Nikolai, in his adulthood, was actually an experience that I had in my own childhood, and was my first sudden, and traumatic, recollection of Atlantis. I was probably about four years old at the time, maybe even three, because I recall that my mother would still occasionally pick me up. We had gone to the Museum of Natural History, and as we were walking through the various hallways and approached the Hall of Ocean Life, I remember seeing the long golden squid that was the only prominently displayed creature in the dimly lit hallways before the ominously dark, huge rectangular entryway to what I came to call "the whale room." It has since sadly been remodeled, brightened up, and Disneyfied. Back in those days, it had a menacingly Neptunian cathedral gloom to it. As we started walking through the entryway, from which the head of the gigantic blue whale suspended from the ceiling could be seen, the entryway which would lead to the top of the stairway descending into the Hall of Ocean Life, with its various sea creature dioramas around an empty square beneath the whale, I began to pull my mother's arm in an increasingly panicked manner, telling her that I did not want to go into the chamber. She picked me up and carried me in anyway. Once we entered the chamber, I saw something so terrifying that I blacked out.

The next thing that I remember is crying at the door to my Persian grandmother's apartment back in Queens (in the same high-rise building that we lived in). I recall walking into her apartment and her asking what had happened and why I was crying. I know that I lost about an hour and a half, because that is about how long it would have taken for us to leave the Natural History Museum, get down to Penn Station, and take the Long Island Rail Road back to Flushing station, which was our usual route when I would visit my mother at her office in the Garment District and my father had the Cadillac with him.

I went back to the Museum of Natural History many times after that. In fact, it was my favorite place throughout my early childhood. But my parents (usually my mother) would not let me go back to the Hall of Ocean Life. One time, when my uncle Richard was visiting from San Francisco, and he took me to the museum while my parents were at work, I insisted on being taken back to the Hall of Ocean Life. He grudgingly agreed. This time I was not scared at all, but I did become obsessed with the fact that the blue whale that was hanging from the ceiling was not the same whale that I had seen that day. I remembered, quite distinctly, seeing a white sperm whale suspended against the background of a night sky.

I made my uncle speak to clerk after clerk, administrator after administrator, demanding to know what had happened to the other whale that used to be in the room. They told me that before the late '60s, there had been a grey whale there, but I knew my whales, as well as I knew my dinosaurs at that age, and a grey whale looks a bit like a blue whale but neither of them looks anything like a sperm whale. I would keep up this routine with my mother on subsequent visits to the museum around the ages of four and five. In fact, I started to suspect that the sperm whale was being hidden in one of the huge warehouses in the museum and I wanted to find out which one.

Many years later, when I met Emma, I would be able to reconstruct what flood of memories, triggered by the atmosphere and the suspended blue whale, must have traumatized me when I was first carried into that room. The image, in *Faustian Futurist*, of my holding hands with her previous Atlantean incarnation as a tsunami wave breaks over the megalithic metropolis and tosses a sperm whale into the night sky above us is an actual memory among the fragments of anamnesis relevant to Atlantis that resurfaced in the early years of my relationship with her. Another part of the same memory is that there had already been an organized, albeit somewhat frantic, exodus of most of the ruling class to predesignated places of refuge around the world. But I had chosen to stay, effectively to commit suicide amidst the destruction of Atlantis, in part because I could not take her with me to one of these bunker-like enclaves, and in part because I wanted to experience the destruction that we had so desperately longed for and which, at the time, I believed would be the baptism of a new beginning.

Later, in my adolescence and early teenage years, I began to have vivid but disjointed memories of walking around this city of Atlantis, while repeatedly hearing the words "the future past" in my mind. In one of these memories, I was on some elevated walkway that led to a building with restricted access, inside of which there were certain mysterious contraptions and elegant devices. It was a place wherein something between science and magic was being practiced, and I was one of the practitioners. I wrote about it for the first time in my earliest attempt at a novel, written when I was 15, which my father deleted from my computer, and the printed manuscript of which I subsequently burned in Central Park.

This was just before I met Emma, after which many fragmentary memories of our past life in Atlantis together surfaced in both of our minds. Akin to the style of the megalithic building blocks of the Atlanteans themselves, these fragmentary recollections were like pieces of a jigsaw puzzle that fit together. Her fragments fit together with mine. Although it was very hard to get her to talk about what she remembered. It would only surface spontaneously when she was in a trance-like state between sleep and wakefulness, often with her head on my lap. If she became too conscious, she would stop talking about the subject, and my attempts to solicit her to do so met with adamant refusal or a dismissal to the effect that she didn't know what she was talking about. The subject clearly made her uncomfortable, and this was a woman with no particular interest in science fiction, the occult, or prehistory. She certainly was not generating these apparent memories from books she had read or films that she had watched. Again, her memories interlocked with many of mine. In some cases, we would each be seeing the same event in this past life from our own perspective.

One particularly vivid recollection was of waiting for her in one of the city's towers. Presumably it was my apartment, which had a spectacular view. She had to pass through a series of concentric circles of massive megalithic enclosure walls to get to me, at least one of which was heavily guarded. I remember being very nervous about the possibility that she might be stopped for something like "not having the proper papers" or lacking some kind of authorization to enter the city. You see, she was not an Atlantean citizen. We were of vastly different social classes or castes. I have the sense that she was entering the city with the kind of clearance that certain servants had. Our relationship was secret and should it have been discovered, there would have been more than a scandal. My sense was that it was a matter of life and death.

Moreover, the transgression of this relationship, on my part, was connected to some more far-reaching and seditious conspiracy that I was involved in. An atmosphere akin to that of martial law hung over the city, and though I knew that my status would, to some extent, militate against my coming under suspicion so easily, there was a real fear that I might be discovered and arrested for treason. This, all the more so, because we lived in a telepathic society and so those of us who were party to the conspiracy had to guard our "deviant" thoughts against surveillance from members of the establishment. We were planning for some kind of coup that also involved dissident elements of the warrior caste. I remember them gazing at us skeptically, from beneath their brutal brows, like we were dreamers liable to get them killed (or worse) for certain ethereal notions that their mercilessly practical minds, which they had by design, could scarcely comprehend.

I would say that in this life, "Emma" was a slave of some kind, although obviously not of the kind that was bound in chain gangs to work at the stone quarries and such. Those were all men. Well, they were hardly human. I described them in detail in *Faustian Futurist*. Those descriptions are not fiction. I would add that we are dealing with a period of prehistory, potentially tens of thousands of years in the past, when other forms of hominin besides Homo sapiens still existed. It was a Tolkienesque world of Neanderthals, Denisovans, Java Men, Hobbits, and so forth, all coexisting with what would become modern man and with a race of Nordic "giants" (certainly compared to the more short-statured races) with elongated skulls who were the Atlantean ruling class.

I was one of these tall people with an elongated skull. Emma described how I looked in detail once, in a particular memory she had of my misappropriating a space cruiser to take her up into lower Earth orbit so that she could see the planet that she lived on. This was very illegal, an experience forbidden for someone of her caste. At any rate, she described what I looked like in some detail, as she recalled looking down at the Earth out the window of the two-seater craft, then back across the cockpit at me, and then back down over the planet again, with an expression of sheer awe and wonder. She said that I had very large blue eyes, a strikingly chiseled face with exceptionally high cheekbones, a broad forehead, and an elongated skull somewhat fluted on the sides, covered by thick, shoulder-length platinum blond hair. I was wearing a silvery skin-tight suit, which shone and changed hues like the skin of a fish as my muscles moved within it. This is also a memory that I incorporated into the "fictional" narrative of *Faustian Futurist*, although I have provided a bit more detail here. But let me not get ahead of myself and return to my childhood recollections.

There was one other incident in my childhood that, in retrospect, I realized was relevant to the lost world of Atlantis. As a small child, I would often lie on the carpet and draw to pass the time. I recall sometimes having been in a mesmeric state when doing so. One time my parents discovered one of my notebooks, which I would endeavor to hide in my room, and to my embarrassment they found these strange people that I would draw in a setting of futuristic cities but with prehistoric elements as well, such as dinosaurs. The people were androgynous or hermaphroditic. Some of them had various animal appendages. In my child's mind, I remember having conceived of the world that I was drawing as something with elements of *The Jetsons* as well as of *The Flintstones*—both cartoons that I would watch in my preschool years.

I might have been five at the time. Looking at these transhuman transsexuals, they thought I was confused about the sexual difference between men and women, but what is strange is that I distinctly remember thinking that they were really stupid for believing this but that I was going to let them believe it so as to continue to conceal what these drawings were really about. I do not now recall what exactly that was, but I remember that at the time I did know. It was something that I did not want them to find out, and I was prepared to let them believe that I was confused about sex before trying to explain to them that such beings were as real as the archeo-futuristic cityscape they were inhabiting and that I had drawn them from recollection.

When I say that I do not now recall *exactly* what that was, it is not to say that I have no idea whatsoever. On the contrary, I quite clearly recall that, throughout my childhood, I had the sense that I was a secret agent not "from here" and that I was supposed to stay "on mission" without even fully recalling precisely what that mission was.

Almost like a sleeper agent, with his secret identity buried so deep that, since it was occulted even from his own conscious mind, it could not be readily discovered by telepathic adversaries—not until it was too late, and he could afford to fully awaken or be openly activated. I have long had a sense of being a soldier in a Secret War.

This may have even extended to my preverbal infancy. Consider what I've been told about speaking my first words—plural. Not my first word, because it was a whole sentence. Prior to this, no one had ever seen me say anything. It wasn't "mama" or "dada" or anything of the sort. It was "Sir, keep coming." Or, rather, "*Agha, hay biya.*" Since my parents both worked, I spent my preschool days with my Persian grandmother, who knew hardly any English (and who lived in the same building as us), Persian was my first language and was not surpassed by English until after kindergarten. My mother says that she was passing by the door to my room, which was creaked open enough for her to see me sitting cross-legged, "like a Buddha," on a little upholstered stool that I had, wedged in a corner between my bookcase (at that time full of stuffed Muppets) and my dresser drawer. It appeared to her as if I was addressing someone who was in the room, but just out of her sight, behind the partly creaked open door. My first words were addressed, not to my mother, but to this person, who seemed to have been "leaving" (disappearing?) in response to my mother approaching the bedroom door. It is to this person that I said what my mother overheard, "Sir, keep coming." Not "hey you, don't go!" or "hey, stay!" *Sir*, keep coming. What rank did this "Sir" hold?

Then, consider the following childhood dream. It begins with my mother accompanying my schoolmates and me on a "field trip" in a little yellow school bus. It is like one of those field trips that we went on in kindergarten and throughout primary school. This is a literal "field" trip, though, in the sense that where they take us is a huge wheatfield to learn how to go back to being farmers or tillers of the earth. I separate myself from the group and leave both them and my mother behind without any of them noticing. Hiding in the tall wheat stalks, I make my way up some very high hills that are beyond the field and then look back down at it somewhat wistfully, but with the knowledge that I did not really belong with them.

Once I get to the top of the hill, over the ridge, the landscape is totally different. Dead, grey—like the Moon. The only structures are concrete bunkers that look like they belong to a militarized civilization. The only color in the entire landscape is from the dials on brightly lit control panels inside these bunkers and also on the inside of featureless, white egg-shaped vehicles that are lined up along the ridge. People in all-white one-piece skin-tight suits, including gloves and white space helmets, are manipulating the controls inside the bunkers and in the eggs. When they put their helmets on and step into the white eggs, becoming as one with them as bikers do with their motorcycles, these eggs glide gracefully off the edge of the ridge into the sky over the wheatfield.

After I take in this scene, the dream shifts to the abandoned World's Fair grounds of Flushing Meadows Park in Queens, near the place where I lived for the first seven years of my life. It is early evening and against the indigo sky, I see these huge UFOs fly overhead that look like really bright pulsating rainbow-colored Christmas ornaments. As soon as I see them, I know that these are actually the featureless white eggs, but they've been disguised. They are projecting a mesmerizing and potentially inspiring illusion. I start to run through the streets to get home to my mother, who I know is there waiting for me, to tell her excitedly that I was right about them—that they are here, and that they've come, just as I said they would!

In retrospect, my impression is that the wheatfield is the field of the workers in the world, but also a field of dreams. While the people hidden atop the hill—actually people on the Moon, which is what it looked like—created humans on this planet as "tillers of the fields." Some of them want to engineer a Luddite reaction against advanced technology to drive us back into the lifestyle of ignorant farmers in a neo-agrarian quasi-feudal caste society. Being above the field in the dream, they were positioned as "Overseers." But others of them believe that they have come to the point where their own civilization is sterile. With their (Easter) eggs (in the sense of the Easter Bunny and of children's Easter egg hunts) they are trying to bring new life to themselves, to *their* world, by inspiring wonder in us so that we will invent and create things beyond their imagination that they can marvel at. This is why the featureless white eggs from the drab-grey bunker world appear like wonderful multi-colored Christmas lights to us. The fact that they reminded me of Christmas has to do, not with Jesus or anything of the kind, but with Santa Claus and a lie that is a gift — what Plato would call a Noble Lie. It was as if they were trying to catalyze the imagination of mankind to supersede the creative possibilities of their own culture. There were two factions, but of a group that had initially been one people — a singular Breakaway Civilization, now divided against itself. One faction was trying to maintain control, another striving to outgrow itself.

In the dream, I am initially leaving my mother and fellows in this world to return to the world that I am actually from. But by the end of the dream, I realize why I am on a mission in this world in the first place: to help inspire a sense of wonder and vital creativity that my own sterile people have lost to their putative "perfection." The running back "home" to my earthly mother means that *this* is my world now. The other is dead. Only *we* can bring a new life to it, but not by going backward to become like farmers again. How is that for an early childhood dream?

Or consider the precognitive "daydreams" that I would have on the actual school bus that took me to a day camp in the summer between kindergarten and first grade. It was located somewhere between Queens and Long Island, and it was called Les Clochettes or "The Bells" in French. If I remember correctly, they taught French there, among other things, and my parents were trying to prepare me for entering the half-French Fleming School on the Upper East Side of Manhattan that coming fall semester of 1987. (I was at a disadvantage because I was entering a first-grade class full of kids who had already gone to Fleming for kindergarten and preschool.) I do not have many memories from this summer day camp, but I do distinctly recall that on the bus rides, especially on the rides back home, with my face pressed against the glass of the window, I would go to this other time. What I experienced there left me with this overwhelming and profound sadness, to the point where sometimes tears would stream down my face, and when I would get back home, I'd be asked why I looked so sad. Or, it could have been that, for other reasons that we will come to, I was sometimes a very sad child when I was left to myself, and it is this sadness that attuned me to the precognitive visions that I had on that bus ride.

In any case, what I saw was a post-apocalyptic world. It was a world where there were much fewer people than there are now. Some kind of disease, or something attendant to it, had killed a lot of people. It was much more of an empty world. No more crowds. There had been a mass depopulation on account of something that was not just physical destruction, as might be caused by war. (Although, that does not mean that there hadn't also been a lot of war.) Those who were left felt like they were living in a dead world, and they almost wanted to join the departed. They felt like they had been left behind. This was not remote viewing or astral projection, where one sees things — including scenes of the future — from some external vantage point. I connected with my future "memories" of being a person who lived in this time and place. I could see my apartment and the surroundings of my building, of the place where I would be living at that time — the view out the window, and what was around my building.

My window looked down on a playground. I also "remember" passing by its structures, at ground level, on my way to and from the building that I was living in. On the rare occasions that parents would bring any of their children to play at this playground at all, there was nothing of the carelessness and joy that parents bringing their children to a playground still has today. It is as if the parents who brought their kids there were miserable people, and as for the children, they had no future. I was looking at them, feeling as if they were stillborn. They were born into a dead world. There was no future ahead of them. So, it was like people's lives had become a farce.

It was a desolate, decimated world of abandoned people. There was a crisis of meaning. People didn't have anything to believe in anymore. They had lost their religion. What oriented their lives had been hollowed out. They had lost their moral compass. A lot of people thought to themselves, "Why are we even still alive? Why *us*?" So many people had died that they were asking themselves, "Why are *we* the ones left?" Though you might think that if there were so few people left, the survivors would be much more tightly knit, that was not the case. On the contrary, there was massive alienation. It is as if society itself had been destroyed. The social fabric had been shredded and people were all isolated, atomized, demoralized, and dissociated, each keeping to themselves, almost as if their apartments were prison cells.

I felt like it was part of my mission to stop this future from materializing. It was in 1987 that I was seeing this, and it seemed like the far future. But if you were to ask me today (in 2022) how far we are from the world that I glimpsed on those bus rides as a child, I would say maybe another twenty years at most. Possibly only another fifteen.

In retrospect, I get the sense that, while it is true that a lot of people had died, that is not the only reason why the city was so empty. About a month before the outbreak of the Covid-19 pandemic in 2020, I was sitting in the living room of Lyn Buchanan, the chief trainer for the US government's secret psychic spying program. He told me that his team of remote viewers had seen a future, around the middle of the 21st century, wherein "artificially produced natural disasters" had been used to depopulate Earth down to only 25% of the current population. Of those people who were left, most of them had voluntarily abandoned cities and moved to isolated homesteads in the countryside. He told me that they appeared to be mortified by disease, and that they wouldn't let anyone but their closest friends and family onto their property. Meanwhile, "only bad people still live in the cities." I asked him what he meant by "bad people." Lyn said, "like outlaws, criminals." People who refused to accept the neo-agrarian, post-industrial order that held sway over the countryside. So, maybe there were children playing joyfully somewhere in that world that I saw on those bus rides. But not in the cities. Rather, as part of a regressive, Traditionalist society of rugged families looking after their own kind. In a way, this connects back to the vision of the workers in the field in the dream about the field trip to teach us how to become farmers again.

Another rather remarkable dream that I had in early childhood was a recurring nightmare of having my right arm bitten off by a black dog. This was around the age of five. I am in a bright yellow raincoat, of the kind that little children wear, standing on a boat next to the jetty of a dock. I am coming in from stormy seas, under an ominous cloudy grey sky shot through with bolts of lightning, hearing thunderclaps all around me. The weather is hot and humid, as if it is summer. Then, this black hound comes up and jumps onto the boat from the wooden dock. It takes my right hand into its mouth and bites into my arm. I can feel an intense burning sensation in my right arm as the hound bites through it, severing my arm and spraying bright red blood all over the yellow raincoat. This nightmare repeated for at least several nights in a row, perhaps even for a whole week. There was a sense of déjà vu and inevitability to the severing of my arm, each time it took place on these successive nights.

I had no idea what this dream meant until many years later, when I was researching the connection between the Indo-European folklores of Iran and Scandinavia, both of which are lands of my ancestors. I am about a quarter Norse, specifically Norwegian. So, the Vikings are among my forebears. As I pointed out in *World State of Emergency* (2017), the Norse god Tyr, who is older than Thor and was doubled in some ways when Thor entered the pantheon, is the oldest Norse deity associated with lightning and thunder. The wolf Fenrir, one of the sons of Loki, whose unbinding signals the end of the world, bites into and severs the right arm of Tyr. Significantly, this leaves Tyr with only his left hand. As in the Left-Hand Path.

The rune for Tyr, who is a war god, is an upward-pointing arrow. Meanwhile, in the ancient Iranian pantheon, "Tyr" means arrow and is the root of the name of "Tyrgan" or the Mithraic holiday of the summer solstice, when people prayed to the dog star for heavy rains to come with thunder and lightning. "Tyr" also refers specifically to *the* arrow of "Arash," the archer, a cognate of the Greek "Ares" and also symbolically equivalent to Orion (Ariyan). In Iranian epic lore, as preserved by the *Avesta*, Arash shoots an arrow that defines the realm of the Aryans (Aryana, or Iran) in distinction from the non-Aryan realms (An-Iran). He is essentially an avatar of Mithra, who is a titan. In the Hindu branch of the Indo-European family, the titans, who are demonized by the Hindus but revered by the Iranians, are associated with the antinomian and taboo-breaking "left-hand path" of Tantra, which is said to only be appropriate for those with a warrior spirit (*vira*). Once the Romans encountered the Norse, they equated Tyr with Mars. Meanwhile, the consort of Mithra, Anahita, is the ancient Iranian goddess of the waters.

In sum, this recurring nightmare drew from the collective unconscious or "genetic memory" of two of my ancestral peoples, plunging to the depth of their shared Indo-European matrix, in order to produce an image of me as Tyr or Mithra. While the thunder and lightning are imagery from the myth of Tyr, together with the hound biting my right arm, the yellow raincoat is the brightness of the sun signifying Mithra in the guise of Sol Invictus—the light that keeps shining amidst stormy darkness. The choppy seas all around me evoke imagery associated with the consort of Mithra, Anahita, whose ruined stone temple in the countryside of the Pars province of Iran I was to make a pilgrimage to many years later. Also, unbeknown to many classicists, it is the Cilician pirates who mainly brought Mithraism to Rome, by way of the sea and through the port cities of the empire.

It is worthy of note, in this regard, that by that age, when I was around five or six, I was already obsessed with traditional Iranian music and would make my Persian grandmother (with whom I spent my days prior to first grade) put it on all the time, despite her pretty much hating it. I had also seen *Conan the Barbarian* by the age of six, and the epic music that Basil Poledouris had composed for that Robert E. Howard saga resonated in my blood in the same way as the music of Shahram Nazeri, Mohammad Reza Shajarian, and the divine Parisa. Speaking of Robert E. Howard, my other quarter (what is left after the 50% Persian and 25% Norse) is Celtic ancestry.

Let me not neglect to mention that the imagery of the black dog, which found its way into the heart of both *Faustian Futurist* and my essay on Kafka (in *Lovers of Sophia*), is also highly significant in the context of the cult of Artemis. Not only was the dog a companion of Artemis in her guise as the huntress, black dogs in particular were sacrificed to Artemis. As I later discovered in my research on ancient Iran, *Artâ-Ameshâ,* or "Immortal Truth," was originally an Iranian goddess of the form of Mithraism practiced by the Sarmatians, a matriarchal northern Iranian tribe of barbarians who became the basis for the Greek "Amazon" legends when the Hellenes encountered them in various areas around the Black Sea, including at Ephesus, where these "Amazons" built the first Temple of Artemis, which became one of the seven wonders of the ancient world and the eventual place of refuge and self-exile for the philosopher Heraclitus (after he sided with the Persian Empire against the democracy of his fellow countrymen, whom he considered an ignorant mob). Artemis and her Amazons were the first women who captured my imagination.

Around the age of six or seven, I went with my father to visit the Metropolitan Museum of Art for the first time. Unlike the Natural History Museum, the MET is not a place frequented by children who are that young. The experience I had there, on that first visit, was almost as powerful as the one with the white whale at the Museum of Natural History. I am talking about encountering the golden statue of Artemis or Diana, as the Archer and Huntress, at the center of a glass-enclosed neo-classical courtyard. I was absolutely transfixed by this idol. The goddess seduced me to the core of my being, a depth at which I recognized her to be the deity to which I was most devoted. It is no wonder that she winds up featuring so prominently in "Trial Goddess," my essay on Kafka (in *Lovers of Sophia*), or the first chapter of *Iranian Leviathan* on the "Mithraic Mother of Iran," and even in *Faustian Futurist* through the esoteric symbol of the black dog sacrifice.

Who knows if one can legitimately suppose that my being a fan of *Wonder Woman* had something to do with my reaction to seeing that statue for the first time, or whether—as I suspect is more likely—a relationship to Artemis and her Amazon devotees that had developed in me many lifetimes ago was the basis for my affinity both for the superheroine and the golden idol of the goddess. In any case, I am sure that they were mutually reinforcing. Seeing that statue at the MET and learning of the historical reality of the Amazons, as depicted in Greek art, probably brought the world of *Wonder Woman* even more vividly to life for me than Linda Carter beating up jack-booted Nazis, or binding them with her "Lasso of Truth," on the daytime TV reruns that I watched religiously throughout my preschool and kindergarten years.

Another show that I was watching in the same years, just as religiously, was the original series of *Star Trek*. In kindergarten, I was already spending considerable time aboard the Starship Enterprise, "boldly going where no man had gone before" with Kirk, Spock, and McCoy. Reruns of the program would air at midnight, and I would insist that my father set up his VHS machine to automatically record them so that I would have them to watch when I got home from school the next day. Once I had my father get the '80s *Star Trek* films for me on VHS as well. One character, besides the main crew, that cut across both the TV series and the greatest of these films made an indelible impression on me: Khan Noonien Singh. In the Original Series episode *Space Seed*, Kirk explicitly compares Khan to John Milton's Lucifer, who considers it "better to reign in hell than serve in heaven." Then, in *Star Trek II*, while vengefully pursuing the Enterprise as if it is his white whale, Khan liberally quotes Captain Ahab more than once:

> He tasks me, and I shall have him.
> I'll chase him round the moons of Nibia
> And round the Antares maelstrom
> And round perdition's flames
> Before I give him up!
>
> …To the last, I grapple with thee.
> From hell's heart, I stab at thee.
> For hate's sake, I spit my last breath at thee.

You might ask how I ever saw *Star Trek* in the first place, if in the '80s reruns of the series only aired in the middle of the night. That is because my parents would sometimes have such terrible fights that I would be up way past my bedtime, with my father letting me watch TV as a way to calm down after being traumatized by throwing myself into the middle of these rather brutal confrontations. If it had not been for my repeated interventions of quick-witted reasoning and penetratingly empathetic mediation, my mother would not have survived my childhood.

When I was still very young, I would sometimes try to sleep between my parents, in their bed, on nights after I had managed to defuse their fights, to make sure that they wouldn't start fighting again. On one of these nights in November of 1989, my mother had fallen asleep, and her head was turned away from the window. My father was still awake, and so was I. All of a sudden, somewhere between 2 and 3 o'clock in the morning, as we were both facing the window and could see the sky very clearly, the sky blew up into rainbow colors. This explosion lasted for about forty seconds, and yet there was no sound whatsoever. Perfect silence. Even the random night noises of

Manhattan couldn't be heard (we were only on the third floor). The window we were looking out of faced east, and so the patch of sky wherein the clouds exploded with this succession of every color in the rainbow was somewhere over the East River. The lights were so intense that they were clearly reflected on the white wall of the room, opposite the windows. My father and I looked back and forth between the explosion itself and its reflection, then at each other, wide-eyed, as if to wordlessly say, "*Are you seeing what I'm seeing?!*"

We were so disturbed that we got out of bed and went into the living room, so as not to wake up my mother, while my father turned on the handheld radio that he kept by his bedside and scanned the channels for any news report about what had just happened. When we heard nothing, we expected that it would at least get coverage the next day. Surely, even at such a late hour, hundreds of New Yorkers ought to have seen it. But there was never any coverage of anyone who reported witnessing such a spectacle.

I remember that it was two or three weeks after the fall of the Berlin Wall on November 9, 1989—an event that I watched live and that made a big impression on me. I even remember connecting the two events that night, wondering if a coup had taken place in the USSR and some rogue Soviet commander had launched a nuclear missile that was intercepted at high altitude on its descent toward New York City. The explosion was *that* dramatic, and those who have actually witnessed mushroom clouds know that remaining fissile material does produce rainbow colors as it burns off after the primary detonation. But it turns out that it was not a hushed-up nuke interception.

Many years, later I learned that there *had* been other witnesses that night. As I wrote about at length in *Closer Encounters* (2021), on the night of November 30, 1989, a mass UFO abduction took place in New York City, centered on the East River front of Manhattan. A whole high-level convoy of dignitaries who had been crossing the Brooklyn Bridge at the time, and whose cars were stalled by the typical electromagnetic effect of the UFOs, had close encounters. Consequently, it is sometimes also called the Brooklyn Bridge Encounter. Among those abducted was none other than the Secretary General of the United Nations, Javier Pérez de Cuéllar, together with at least twenty other people, some of whom were levitated into craft after passing straight through their closed apartment building windows into the night sky over the East River. It was at exactly that time, between 2 and 3 AM, that my father and I saw the lights. Would *I also* have been abducted had I not been sleeping in my parents' bed on one of my many night watches to prevent bloody murder?

How much of what I wrote about the murder/suicide of Nikolai's parents in *Faustian Futurist* is a projection from traumatic terror that I suffered in this lifetime? I consider it an open question. I do remember that Nikolai was orphaned and that he had been raised by a purported aunt and uncle, but I wonder whether what I wrote about the ultimately murderous domestic abuse was in fact a veridical memory of *how* he was orphaned or whether that is a projection being mixed with actual past life recollections that flooded my mind during and after a walk on the beach at Coney Island in 2005. The connection between Nikolai's psychic ability and the trauma that he endured is also relevant here. You see, I myself developed certain psychic abilities, and had certain paranormal experiences, on account of this home situation.

In my attempt to intervene with the aim of diffusing fights between my parents before my mother was in danger of suffering serious violence, I got into the habit of lying in my bed with an ear pressed to the wall—straining to hear what was going on in my parents' room, which was on the other side of a sizeable living room that separated my room from theirs. No normal human hearing would be able to pick up a conversation across the distance in question, not in that style of an apartment. But, over time, I noticed that I was actually able to do so. My hearing became preternaturally powerful, to the point that I could pick up a conversation even in hushed tones, at that distance, with their door closed, and know whether it was the kind of "conversation" that could lead to a fight. I tested this theory a number of times, entering their room when I thought a fight might be about to begin, only to find that the demeanor, tone, and body language of my parents clearly confirmed this.

I had developed what parapsychologists call clairaudience. This actually became somewhat of a nuisance. In places like crowded restaurants, I began to tune in to one or another conversation taking place around me and hear each of them in such great detail that I had trouble focusing on what was happening at my own table or the conversation that I myself was engaged in.

One night in bed, as my ear was pressed to the wall, trying to listen across the house, I fell through the wall and into the living room. The wall felt cold as my body passed through it, and I rolled onto the carpet of the living room, right under where one of those two Persian paintings that I described in *Uber Man* was hanging on the wall. It was the middle of the night, so it should have been dark in the living room, but there was a strange dim bluish light that made it possible to see everything in the room fairly distinctly. It was not the light of the predawn hour, because the view out the windows was still black as midnight.

As soon as I got my bearings in the living room and got back up on my feet, this ethereal visibility was sufficient for me to make out a jet-black spectral hound in the opposite corner of the room. It was too dark and shadowy a thing for me to tell whether it was a dog or a wolf. The thing began to chase me around the living room. Running from it, I fell over the arm of the white sofa and onto the couch pillows — face down. I have never felt anything more terrifying in my life than the moment that the spectral hound jumped onto me and entered me through my lower back. The next thing I knew, I was in my bed again, shocked. The experience was some paradoxical cross between a horrifying rape, with an appalling loss of rational willpower, and empowerment by some superhuman — or inhumanly powerful — alien thing.

Around the age when this happened, and for some time after, I was fascinated by the black Spider-Man, and one point of comparison for the thing that fused with me could be the alien symbiote "suit" that is no mere suit when it turns Spider-Man black. Not to go on too long of a tangent, but this brings something else to mind, from much later in my life, which I omitted from *Uber Man*.

In the very early morning hours of one day in the Spring of 2018, I woke up to see a huge tarantula in the center of the wooden floor of my bedroom. It was so real that my first thought, actually my thoughtless first reaction, was to grab my laptop (with all of my data on it!) to throw down onto the spider so as to crush it — since I was at a loss to find anything else on the desk near my bed that would be big enough or heavy enough to do so. Just as I was about to throw the laptop onto the thing, it slowly began to fade away while moving its hairy legs back and forth in a fixed position on the floor. About six months later, having moved to a different apartment, another spectral spider materialized on my wall early one morning. This one was a huge daddy longlegs, spanning the entire length of the molding separating the ceiling from the wall. It slowly made its way across this molding, rounded a corner in the wall, and only began to dissolve as it walked into a patch of bright sunlight streaming in through my venetian blinds. I was wide awake the whole time. Later, I found out that on the same day that I had this second spider experience, my future fiancée, Nassim Nouri, had been standing under huge sculptures of spiders on display at an art museum in San Francisco. She has a photograph, with the menacing spider legs towering over her, time-stamped to the same date as I cryptically posted the symbol of the black Spider-Man to my Facebook after my second encounter.

The Marvel superhero that is most relevant to my experience with the spectral hound is not Spider-Man, though. It is actually the Incredible Hulk. Another show that I watched from earliest childhood was *The Incredible Hulk* live-action series, which also got me into collecting comic books (the first comics that I collected were of the Hulk).

As a child, I was strangely fixated on *Frankenstein*, to the point where I tried to read Shelley's novel of *The Modern Prometheus* at the age of six. It was the first adult book that I made an attempt to understand, poring over it for hours, with a dictionary by my side, and sometimes by candlelight, as if it were a sacred occult text whose enigmas I had to decipher. So, I already connected Dr. Banner to Dr. Frankenstein and the Hulk to the monster born of his titanic ambition. But the Hulk was also born of something else.

The good doctor would transform into the monster when he was overcome by powerlessness, fear, and anger in the face of brutalization—of himself or someone he loved, cared for, and wanted to protect from unjust harm. In the TV series, this made the kind-hearted scientist an alienated outsider and perpetual fugitive traveling under aliases, one who had let himself be presumed dead. In the comic books, he is a product of the Military-Industrial Complex who turns against them—twisting the gun barrels and smashing the tanks of those who presume to have authority by wielding state power. For years, I deeply identified with Dr. Banner and the Hulk, and I think that it is something like the preternatural and pre-rational power of the Hulk that entered me that night during my astral projection to the living room. A power of transformation that, much later, in my early twenties, was more explicitly symbolized by the terrifyingly shamanic Wolf Man dream that I related in *Uber Man*. The one wherein I am turned into an instrument of my future self by the pinstripe-suited werewolf living in the stone castle in the forest. A dream that was then but a dark prophecy but is now unfolding as a reality.

The reason why I mentioned the traumatic incidents of my childhood in the context of discovering *Star Trek* is that I suspect that the trauma I endured broke open my mind—and heart—to an exceptionally profound internalization of the mythic and religious elements embedded in the science-fictional narratives of American popular culture. Having been raised by two totally secular parents, and finding that far more than them, I myself always contemptuously despised the extant organized religions, my nonetheless profound sense of the sacred sought out this spectacular wellspring. Had my father simply been an angry and abusive brute, I might not have been put in such a receptive state with respect to these archetypally Promethean narratives and symbols in American pop culture. It was because he could also act so loving and caring, and because he was such an entrancing story-teller, that his assaults actually made me question everything about reality so deeply—from what love is, to what legitimates authority, and what counts for knowledge.

The world of Marvel and DC superheroes battling supervillains, the Jedi and Sith in *Star Wars* struggling over their use of the Force, *Star Trek*, including and especially *The Next Generation* that aired throughout my childhood, the first two *Terminator* films, the *Ghostbusters* films, and *The Real Ghostbusters* animated series—these metanarratives opened cosmic spaces and psychic realms up for my exploration of deeply disturbing existential questions. By the age of ten, in 1991, I had already accepted time travel, space aliens, mutants, genetic supermen, destroyed super civilizations, robots, ghosts, reincarnation, and psychic super powers into my worldview, but coupled with a contemptuous rejection of anything like God Almighty. gods, like Gozer or Darkseid. Yes—although we ought to *become* them through our own techno-scientific power, rather than worship them. God? Hell *no*! I suspected that if there *were* a God, he would at best be some manipulative, and borderline abusive, trickster like Q in *Star Trek: The Next Generation*.

My appreciation for science fiction also translated into an actual childhood affinity for science. I won first prize at the Science Fair of the Fleming School three years in a row. It was sometime during this stretch, probably when I was around the age of 8 (in 1989), at the beginning of the third grade, that I started to have recurring nightmares about being an old man living out of suitcases in a hotel room. I call them nightmares, rather than simply dreams, because whenever I would wake up from these, I would be filled with a sense of the most forlorn and lonely sadness, to the point that sometimes tears would be streaming down my cheeks.

One morning I tried to tell my parents about these dreams, but they did not understand what I was saying. As I recall, my father did not say very much, other than to be annoyed by how insistently I latched onto something that he considered morbid. As for my mother, she said something to the effect that "you'll never wind up like that." I tried to explain to her that this was the past, and that I had wound up like that, because I had already been that old man. I believe she may have asked whether the person I was describing was a traveling salesman, to which I answered that he was not, because even a traveling salesman has a home that he goes back to, eventually, whereas this old man had no home. He moved everything that he had to his name with him, in suitcases, from hotel to hotel. I recall describing him as having been "homeless" in a sense because of this. My father did not like that.

These dreams took place over the course of a number of nights, and I still recall quite a few vivid details from them. At one point, I was pulling the loose skin on my old face so that it was tight enough to be able to shave in the bathroom mirror. I also saw myself standing in front of a full-length mirror, pulling the belt on my pants tight enough so that it would keep them up, because I had become so emaciated that my old suits no longer fit me. I had a limp and was using a cane. I recall that this was the result of an accident wherein I was hit by the front metal bumper grills of an old New York taxi cab. There were witnesses to the accident, and they wanted me to go to the hospital. From one of the dreams, I recall that I refused because I was afraid that I would be humiliated if people found out that I was too poor to be able to afford to pay the hospital bills. They knew who I was, as if I had been famous at one point, and they would be as shocked as I would be ashamed if they discovered that this public figure had reached the point of such destitution. Not just poverty, but also loneliness. There wasn't anyone who I could really turn to for help. I remember strolling in a small park and feeding pigeons. Actually, I felt like a penned-in prisoner.

There were a couple of images that eventually served as a basis to identify the place and time that the dream was set in. One recurring image was of sitting in a diner attached to the lobby of the hotel, where I would order something like a grilled cheese sandwich and beer. Always something soft because my teeth were falling out. I even remember the part of the diner that I sat in. It was one of the small tables in the row of seats on the side that faced the sidewalk of 34th street headed from 8th toward 9th avenue. I identified the location a year or two after having had the dreams, when I was walking through the Garment District, where my mother worked, and we went into the Hotel New Yorker. There is a plaque dedicated to Nikola Tesla on exactly *that* side of the New Yorker, outside the wall of the Tick Tock Diner that has been restored and is still there today.

I also identified the lobby of the hotel (attached to the diner) from another scene in this dream, which was quite enigmatic to me when I first dreamt about it. In this scene, I am sitting on leather upholstered furniture in the lobby and next to me there is this filthy copper bowl-like thing that is raised on some kind of stand or tripod. There was more than one of these, with some of them further from where I was sitting. The interior of the bowl was full of dark stains, to the point where the copper or bronzish-colored metal was barely visible. Neither of my parents knew what this thing could have been. Later on, I described it to "Nana," my American great-grandmother, and she blurted out, "Well, that's a spittoon!" I said, "A what?" She explained how when she was young, they used to be everywhere and were for men to spit their chewing tobacco out into. Apparently, the lobby of the Hotel New Yorker once featured these as well.

While I was able to identify the New Yorker as the hotel from the dreams, I did not realize that the old man was Nikola Tesla until much later. In the 1980s, during my childhood, Nikola Tesla had been relegated to obscurity as far as the general public was concerned. Only people in the engineering and physics communities remembered him. It was not until the early years of the 21st century that Tesla began to be rediscovered, and it is only very recently that people have been allowed to remember the scale of his contribution. We certainly were not taught about him in school back when I was a kid. I was able to make the identification when a second set of memories from the life of Tesla flashed through my mind in 2005 at the age of 24.

These were from much earlier in that life. In one of them, I remembered walking through the streets of Manhattan at night with a dossier folder under my arm. The streets were much darker than they are now. The street lights were fewer and far between. I had just left a meeting wherein I was presenting what was in the portfolio to a group of businessmen seated around a boardroom table. Inside that leather portfolio holder under my arm were the drawings and schematics that I had set before these men. Black and white images of electrified power-broadcasting towers and sleek, wingless aerial vehicles gliding through the sky, and others of unconventional submarines. All of them looked like something out of science fiction. As I walked through the streets, I was worried. I had the distinct impression that the men I had just met with thought I was crazy. That they had stared at me like I was a wild-eyed mad scientist and had only humored me the way one humors someone senile or an inmate at a mental institution. *They think I'm a madman, and they're not going to fund me*, I was thinking to myself.

Another memory, from an even earlier period, was very emotionally intense. It involved losing my mother from that lifetime. I recalled that we had been very close, and that I had a deep sense of guilt for "abandoning" her back home when I went from my studies abroad to becoming an immigrant in America to pursue my life's work. Now word had reached me, way too late, that she was dying and wanted me by her bedside. I remember rushing back to Europe, panic-stricken that I might not make it back to her in time to say goodbye. But I did, just barely.

The most interesting memory of this set, though, came once more in dreams, and it offered some kind of external validation. At that time, I had met a young Parisian woman who was studying journalism and drama at New York University. She was taking the same graduate Philosophy seminar that I was. Actually, I wasn't enrolled in the class. I used to sit in on it. Thomas de Zengotita, my mentor from The Dalton School was the teacher. It was a graduate course on Heidegger and Wittgenstein, which I had already taken as an undergrad. But I would often sit in again to brush up on *Being and Time*. Very shortly after meeting Marie, and developing a magnetic rapport with her, I began to dream of her as a theater performer in an Art Nouveau kind of setting. In these dreams, I would call her "Sarah" and she would bring me backstage to keep her company either before or after her performances.

One time, as Marie and I were taking a long stroll together through The Ramble in Central Park, I told her about these dreams. She looked at me like I had just been caught going through her dresser drawers or something. Then, with the forthrightness that was characteristic of our rapport, she proceeded to tell me some very intimate things about her life, which I will not repeat here, but which had led her to strongly suspect that she was the reincarnation of Sarah Bernhardt. "The Divine Sarah," as she had been known during the years when she became the greatest female actress in the history of Western drama, was a very close friend and confidant of Nikola Tesla. They had met in Paris, following his graduate studies in Prague. After he moved to New York, Tesla would invite her to hang out with him at his series of laboratories.

The only other person that close to Tesla was Mark Twain. Speaking of which, after I realized that Marie was Sarah, I began to suspect that Warren Lubetkin, with whom I used to love playing Mad Scientist as a child, and who for a time was really into the writings of Samuel Clemens, was probably "Mark Twain" reincarnated. My childhood obsession with Doctor Frankenstein and his electrified laboratory also started to make a lot more sense to me. By the way, "Victor" (as in Frankenstein) and Nikola are synonyms. "Frankenstein" means Truthful Stone, in reference to the "philosopher's stone" of the alchemists (Dr. Frankenstein is the last great alchemist). So "Victor Frankenstein" could be rendered as "Nikola Philosopher Stone."

The last of the images in the second set of memories from the life of Tesla is also relevant to my past life memories of having been an Atlantean. One fine day in the Spring of 2005, while sitting in my room intently contemplating the *Yoga Sutras of Patanjali*, I was suddenly struck with a vivid image of an operational World Wireless tower. But it was not the prototype built by Tesla in Colorado, nor was it the one that he tried to build in Shoreham, Long Island, until J. P. Morgan pulled the funding for it. Rather, this fully operational tower, shooting bolts of lightning through the night sky, was of a piece with the aesthetic style of the high-precision megalithic architecture surrounding it in Atlantis. At that moment I realized that I had not *invented* World Wireless. With my high-fidelity three-dimensional photographic memory, I had *remembered* and *copied* it. How many other "inventions" of mine were pieces of Atlantean technology?

As I already intimated in *Uber Man*, albeit without going into as much detail, these memories from the life of Tesla were the basis for what I wrote about him in *Faustian Futurist*. But there is something else about the life, or rather, about the slow death of Tesla that I was trying to get at in *Faustian Futurist* but that I was only subsequently able to fully piece together. In *Faustian Futurist*, I depict the elder Tesla at the New Yorker Hotel as a prisoner of OSS agents who were actually operatives of Nazi Germany. They had set him up to be stripped of citizenship, and potentially charged with treason, by forging that Amtorg Trading Corporation contract (dated to Hitler's birthday) that he signed, thinking that he was handing the Death Ray over to the Soviet Union to defeat the Nazis, since he had already unsuccessfully tried to sell it to the Allied Powers. I suggested that these OSS agents went so far as to take out rooms on the same floor of the hotel as him, the 33rd floor, where they proceeded to quickly move certain items of his — I mean of my — things to their room immediately after my death and before the hotel staff was allowed to discover my body. But the most haunting scene is one where the group of Nazi double agents posing as OSS men turns out to be led by a Ukrainian woman, Nikita, who becomes Nikolai's aunt. The suggestion is made that she traps Tesla's soul, my soul, forcing me to reincarnate as "Nikolai Alexandrov" — the tortured and short-lived protagonist of *Faustian Futurist*. The implication is that Tesla was the target, not just of espionage, but also of surveillance or even capture that extended to the psychotronic level.

If Nikola Tesla, who was well versed in occult subject matters, whose favorite book was *Faust* and who was personal friends with Swami Vivekananda, wanted to find a way to protect what was inside of his mind, how would he have done it? What would I have done with all the technological plans and unwritten patents, or background for interpreting patents, that were locked inside the vault of my mind? Only recently did I realize why I have always had the impression that Tesla was not himself for a long stretch toward the end of his life, and why, the older he got, the more pieces of him seemed to be missing. It is because I sent parts of my soul away like carrier pigeons. I fragmented myself, storing certain parts of my knowledge and capacities in multiple individuals to be born in the future. This is how I intended to escape the capture that Nikolai was subjected to, or at least to hide certain information from the captors. The "soul" is like software. It can be copied, and its code can also be split. It is not some indestructible and self-identical essence. There is no *atman*. Tesla understood this at least implicitly. It is one of the reasons why he found Buddhist metaphysics and epistemology so compelling that he sent copies of *The Gospel of Buddha* (1894) by Paul Carus to all of his close friends.

Despite my general contempt for organized religion, I do admit that, in this lifetime as well, the religion for which I've had the most respect is Buddhism. My longstanding appreciation for Japanese culture has probably been one reason for that. This appreciation for Japan began at the Fleming School with several convergent trajectories. Firstly, like many American kids in the 1980s, I grew up playing the original Nintendo and I was impressed by the imaginative and creative power of the Japanese, who developed the worlds of these video games. I also got to play the Super Nintendo, or as it was called in its Japanese version, the Super Famicom, almost a year before it came out in the United States. There was a kid in my homeroom at Fleming who drew explosions and other ultra-violent and sometimes also sexual imagery that occasionally landed him in the principal's office. He was a loner, and few kids would talk to him. He didn't say much himself. I was intrigued and engaged with him, accepting his invitation to come over to his house. It turned out that he was the son of a very wealthy executive, who often traveled to Japan for business, bringing back all of the latest toys, videos, and tech for his son. In those days, for a brief period in the late 1980s, Japan was surpassing America in innovation and there were even short-lived fears of a Japanese economic takeover of the United States. (If only it *had* been Japan, rather than China.)

This brings me to the second trajectory to my appreciation of Japanese culture, which was Japanese anime. This kid showed me all kinds of sci-fi/horror cartoons that were inappropriate for children, from the film *Akira* and the original Japanese version of the series censored as *Voltron* in the US, namely *Go Lion*, to *Goku Midnight Eye*, *Mad Bull 34*, and even *Angel Cop*. I watched these spectacles of Satanic spectrality, wondering how the same culture that produced them could have also developed a discipline such as Judo.

I took up that martial art, first at the Fleming School, and then much more seriously at the Kyushu Dojo of Ryohei and Rusty Kanokogi. I would commute for over an hour each way, from Manhattan to Flatbush Avenue, Brooklyn, then one of the most dangerous neighborhoods in New York. Despite being the only white kid in a class of thirty blacks (with one Hispanic), I was never once taunted or bullied by anyone in the Dojo. In fact, the Kanokogis had turned their African-American students into neighborhood crime fighters. The local criminals were afraid of Kyushu Dojo and its plain-clothes attendees. That was the power of discipline, order, and cohesion cultivated by Japanese culture prevailing over some of the worst elements of American society.

That stayed with me. By the time I interviewed for entry to the Dalton School in fifth grade—a month into the school year, when Fleming had suddenly gone bankrupt and unexpectedly closed its doors—Japan already featured prominently in the vision of world order that I laid out in front of the interviewer. It was 1992, a year after the fall of the Soviet Union, and so I said to her that now we had an opportunity to unify the entire north of the planet, from NATO through Russia *and including Japan*, not only by means of economic and political treaties, but also by building an inter-continental system of maglev bullet trains of the kind that they were then starting to build in Japan. What it was about Japan that could yield both the discipline of Judo and also the insanely creative visions of Japanese anime, as well as the country's productive power in technological innovation, convinced me that Japan was key in laying the groundwork for the kind of United Earth that I wanted to see as a springboard for space colonization. I told the interviewer that Dalton should bring back Japanese language classes, because I wanted to add this language to my knowledge of French and Persian. Well, I got in. (It helped that Dustin Hoffman's son Jake was out for a year, on a set with his father in Hollywood. He was quite miffed when he came back to see that I'd taken his place, and his father had to "donate" more to get him back in.)

There is something else about Judo that, it occurs to me, connects both to the Promethean aspect of the Japanese psyche and also to why I appreciate the Buddha Dharma more than any of the other major world religions. Unlike Karate and almost every other martial art, Judo is about letting the opponent lean into you and turning his attack into your defense by transforming the energy directed at you. Very much by contrast with the aggressive standoff characteristic of Karate, where one aims to keep the adversary at an arm's (or a leg's) length, on the other side of a blow directed outwards, Judo is about *letting the enemy come into your arms*, under the *illusion* that *he is in control*. If people understood how deep an impact practicing Judo had on me, they would grasp a lot more about what I was trying to do between 2016 and 2018. Training in Judo begins with *learning how to fall*.

What Prometheus does to Zeus, over the long arc of his struggle against Olympus, is essentially a Judo throw—especially one of those where you let the opponent hook your leg out from under you, and while you look like you're going down first, you plant your other leg in his gut and throw him hard over you before rolling over to pin him. If we were dealing only in classical martial arts and setting aside Bruce Lee's brilliant innovation of Jeet Kune Do, then Judo would definitely be the martial art of choice for Prometheus.

Who is Prometheus? Why did I choose him? Or, if it is the other way around, why was I chosen by him? The myth of Prometheus is peculiar insofar as it is the most inexhaustibly meaningful and far-reaching myth in the entire history of mankind, and yet it has been rendered somewhat obscure by comparison to certain other myths. This has probably been by design, because the tremendous meaning of the myth of Prometheus is incomparably more dangerous to established interests than any other tale with archetypal power. The parasitic elite wants you to forget about Prometheus. That, despite the fact that he is the creator, civilizer, and liberator of mankind.

Prometheus is a titan. He is the son of the titans Iapetus and Themis. It is noteworthy in this regard that Themis is herself the daughter of Uranus and Gaia, or Heaven and Earth, and she is the creator of the Oracle at Delphi, which she later gives to Apollo. This is relevant to the power of prophecy that is part of the "forethought" of Prometheus, the quality that defined his name and to which we will return. The titans were a class of divine beings who ruled before the Olympians, until they lost a great battle against these new gods. That cosmic war is referred to as the *Titanomachia* or "clash of the titans (with the gods)."

We find a version of this war in all of the Indo-European cultures. In India it is the war between the Daevas and the Ashuras, with the Ashuras being titans. In the Iranian version, there is an inversion wherein the titans or Ahuras are valorized. In archaic Iran, the most important of these Ahuras is Mithra and later, in the teachings of Zarathustra (circa 600 BC), the name of the most important Iranian deity becomes Ahura Mazda, or the "Titan of Wisdom," and he is associated with an ever-burning fire. Moreover, there is a myth according to which the founder of the Order of the Magi stole cosmic fire from Heaven and established its hearth on Earth, with the Magi as its guardians. Prometheus came to prominence as a tragic hero in Greek culture in the 6th century BC, particularly in the Prometheus Trilogy of Aeschylus (*Prometheus the Fire Bringer*, *Prometheus Bound*, and *Prometheus Unbound*) after the integration of much of Greece into the Persian Empire. Before that, as in the *Theogony* and *Works and Days* of the paternalistic authoritarian bard Hesiod, Prometheus was a cautionary tale warning against defying the divine authority of Zeus and the perennial power of Tradition. As we shall see, there are strong Iranian influences on the symbols of this myth.

To begin with, the imagery of Prometheus waging war against Chronos, the chief of the titans and the Lord of Time, has an older precedent in the struggle of Mithra to overpower Zurvan (Chronos) by surmounting the Earth and grabbing hold of the wheelwork of the celestial sphere so as to free humanity from fatalistic planetary and zodiacal influences. The skull and crossed bones, which was first flown by the Cilician pirates who were devotees of Mithra, was a symbol of overcoming the realm of time and death (with the skull being the head of the defeated Zurvan/Chronos and the bones crossed at 23 degrees symbolizing the intersection of the plane of the zodiac with the celestial equator, suggesting the power of Mithra to move the stars). Prometheus is the archetypal pirate. The titans reject his suggestions of complex strategies, and, with his unmatched power of forethought, he foresees that they will be defeated by the gods on account of a foolish decision to fight by brute force. So, he decides to side with the gods by offering strategic advice to Zeus and helping him to become enthroned on Olympus. Like the angel Lucifer, before he becomes Satan and is banished from Heaven for opposing the Lord Jehovah, Prometheus starts off as God's right-hand man—or perhaps left-hand man would be more appropriate (as in the Left-Hand Path).

Meanwhile, the other defeated titans are bound beneath the Earth in Tartarus, a subterranean realm that later (together with Hades and the Neptunian realm of Poseidon) served as a template for the Christian image of Hell. This included one of the brothers of Prometheus, Menoetius, whose name means "doomed might." He is important because as the titan of hubris, or exceeding pridefulness, and of violent anger and rash action, he symbolizes the shadow or dark side of Prometheus that is later integrated into the image of Satan. The second brother of Prometheus, namely Atlas, has a special punishment reserved for him. As the strongest of the titans and the general who led them all in the *Titanomachia*, instead of being bound in Tartarus, Zeus condemns him to separate Heaven and Earth from one another by bearing the weight of the celestial sphere on his own shoulders. We will come back to the relevance of this to the meaning of the Prometheus myth. The third brother of Prometheus, namely Epimetheus or "after-thought," escapes the wrath of Zeus because he joins Prometheus in siding with the Olympians.

In fact, Epimetheus is entrusted with a very special task. As Plato recounts in his dialogue *Protagoras*, when Zeus rewards Prometheus for his loyalty by allowing the titan to craft the new race of mankind "out of clay," as one of a number of species that are created on the Earth at this time, Epimetheus is afforded the opportunity to help his brother in this monumental task, as a kind of sub-contractor. However, Epimetheus, whose name means "afterthought," is a bit of a bumbling idiot and a forgetful fool who acts before he thinks and only realizes things in hindsight (as compared to the defining "foresight" of Prometheus). So when he gives fur to certain animals to keep them warm in the cold, and claws to other animals to defend themselves, and huge sharp teeth to certain predators to feed on other animals to nourish themselves, and speed to yet others so that they can escape with their lives when confronted by a predator, Epimetheus forgets to endow the men molded out of clay by his brother Prometheus with any essence or capacities that are unique to them and that would let them fend for themselves amidst Nature's savagery.

Prometheus remedies this in two ways, and they are both terribly significant. Firstly, he enlists the aid of Athena, who gives the gift of a soul to mankind in the form of a butterfly. The butterfly is a symbol of metamorphosis, transformation, and freedom. Athena helps Prometheus because it is Prometheus who used an axe to slice through the "close-knit" (*pykinos*) mind of Zeus in order to deliver Athena from out of his brain (she is birthed from out of his skull). As the goddess of Wisdom and War, in other words, of the inextricability of warfare from the pursuit of wisdom, the symbolism of Athena is also relevant to the meaning of the Prometheus myth, since Prometheus is the one who midwifed her into the world. Secondly, and more famously, Prometheus remedies the forgetfulness of Epimetheus by breaking into the workshop of Hephaestus (the crafts god) on Olympus and stealing the fire of the forge in a fennel stalk torch, racing back to mankind as a thief on the run, and gifting mortals with this stolen fire as "a means to mighty ends." Not only does this fire symbolize *techne* or craft, Prometheus acts as "a teacher in every art," a civilizer who reveals to us knowledge of all of the arts and sciences, and how to use fire for every manner of invention and innovation.

There are a number of very important interpretive points here. Firstly, the fact that at our creation we are left without any essence or nature of the kind that defines all of the other animals means that our existence precedes our essence. In other words, there is no such a thing as "human nature." Let alone a God-given human nature. We were not created by God, but by titans with the qualities of *Promethea* and *Epimethea*, or forethought/foresight and afterthought/hindsight, both of which are reflected in our own behavior. The fact that our lack of essence is remedied only by the gifts of a butterfly for a soul and the fire of *techne* (craft), from which we get the word technology, means that our very existence is defined only by the power to undergo metamorphosis and to transform ourselves, like a caterpillar into a butterfly, by means of the power of the arts and sciences—including every form of technology.

This is tremendously liberating, and in this connection, it is important to note that the Statue of Liberty in New York Harbor was designed by Bartholdi to be a representative of Mithra in the second grade of initiation of Mithraism, that of the Nymph (wherein the initiate becomes a transvestite), and insofar as Prometheus is a Greek version of Mithra the torch being defiantly born aloft by Lady Liberty is also intended to evoke the fire stolen by Prometheus. The theft of the fire from Olympus in the form of a fennel torch is the basis for the ceremony of the torch race in ancient Athens, which Plato uses as the opening imagery of his ultra-Promethean treatise *Republic*, and which becomes the inspiration for the ceremony of the torch in the Olympic Games. There was a fire altar to Prometheus in Plato's Academy and people would light torches in its flames and carry them down into the city of Athens.

That Prometheus became the civilizer deity, who taught all of the arts and sciences that eventually became enshrined in the Academy, draws a parallel to the story of the Fallen Angels in Genesis 6 and in the Book of Enoch that was excerpted from this part of the Bible. As these biblical books tell us, these rogue angels under the leadership of Satan, who leads a rebellion of a couple of hundred of them against God, came down and gave mankind the gift of sciences and technologies that had been hidden from them by God and the obedient angels. Both the Prometheus myth and the biblical parallel are probably based on the older Sumerian tale of Enki, the benevolent creator of mankind, who opposes his tyrannical brother Enlil, a storm god like Jehovah, who wants to keep mankind as a slave race living in enforced ignorance. Enki, as a proto-Prometheus, brings seven sages with him on a mission to teach humans all of the arts and sciences that would afford them the potential to determine their own destiny.

The theft of fire was only the first of the cunning machinations that earned Prometheus the epithet of being a "trickster." The second occurred when Zeus came to Prometheus to demand that he determine a form of sacrifice for his creatures to offer up to the Olympian gods as a sign of their subservience. Prometheus tricked Zeus badly. He prepared two bowls, one with marbled fat covering only the white bones of a sacrificed animal, another with the lean meat of the ox stuffed into the displeasing-looking skin of the ox's stomach. Zeus chose the former as the prototype of sacrifice and was enraged to discover that only bones were beneath the alluring and deceptive layer of fat. Thereby Prometheus secured the most nourishing part of the animal for mankind. What this element of the myth really means is that, as in the case of the theft of fire as a means to human enlightenment and self-determination, Prometheus was very intent on giving men the ability to irreverently defy the gods and to live for themselves.

Of course, Zeus couldn't have this. He retaliated by sending a beautiful woman to Epimetheus, the original honey pot as it were, bearing a jar or box that the woman herself was told never to open. Each of the Olympian gods and goddesses had put some kind of ill or misfortune inside this box, from war and pestilence to drought and starvation, and so forth. The woman bearing the gift was named Pandora, meaning "all gifts." Most interestingly, it is said that she was the first woman among the race of men created by Prometheus. In other words, the first men were sexually undifferentiated. If one sets this myth into the context of another Greek myth about sexual differentiation, which we see Plato reference in his dialogue *Symposium*, they were not, strictly speaking, a race of males, but an androgynous race or a species of hermaphrodites. Thus, the arrival of Pandora represents sexual differentiation and suggests that many dangers and miseries are attendant to this loss of sexual wholeness in each individual.

In any case, despite his having been told by Prometheus not to accept any gifts from Zeus, the forgetful fool, Epimetheus, is stunned by Pandora's beauty and accepts her as his wife. For her part, Pandora cannot resist the curiosity of looking into the jar or box. When Pandora's box is opened, every miserable ill and misfortune escapes out into the world of mankind, including everything attendant to sex, lustful passion, tragic romance, matrimonial strife, and so forth. All that remains in the box is *elpis* or "hope" in the sense of desperate faith that things can be other than they are. So, the aspiration for utopia in the midst of a perceived dystopia is also part of the myth of Prometheus.

In fact, this aspiration for utopia has a lot to do with the next act of vengeance that we see from Zeus. Despite his intention to make life impossible for mankind by means of Pandora's box, and through the strife attendant to the division of the race into men and women, the creatures of Prometheus somehow manage to build an ocean-going civilization with very high technology that is on the brink of unifying the whole world under the banner of rebellion against Olympus. What is more, the sovereign of this civilization, a son of Poseidon (who becomes, in his own way, an adversary of Zeus), is named after the brother of Prometheus, the titan Atlas. This links back to Atlas as the one who bears the heavens on his own shoulders, and whose name consequently comes to refer to the star charts, ocean navigation maps, and other atlases, such as even medical atlases, that are part and parcel of mapping out human knowledge and opening up new horizons for intrepid exploration. This is why Plato's story of Atlantis in *Critias* immediately follows his description of the Atlas-like demiurge in *Timaeus*.

Atlantis, or the realm of King Atlas, corresponds to the pre-flood civilization of Genesis populated by hybrids produced from the mating of mortal women with the rebel angels who had come down to teach humans all of the arts and sciences that were meanly hidden from them by God in Heaven. Except that the biblical version has been badly distorted to make it appear as if the same God who brings the worldwide flood to punish the putative hubris of this race of rebellious mortals is the God who sends Noah to build an ark to save certain men and animals from the deluge. The original version, related in the myth of Prometheus, makes much more sense. It is the son of Prometheus, Deucalion, who tries to save what humans he can from the jealous and sadistically controlling Zeus, who is intent on destroying humanity by means of the deluge because if humans will not serve him, then they are better off being exterminated altogether. Deucalion succeeds in preserving human life and, like his father, becomes a civilizer who helps to restore high culture.

What is worse, from the perspective of Zeus, is that Prometheus with his foresight harbors the secret of who is going to overthrow him and take his place as a more just and humanitarian ruler on Olympus. Zeus is intent on prying this secret from out of the mind of Prometheus, so he has Prometheus arrested and bound by Kratos and Bia, or "Power" and "Violence." This symbolism makes clear the character of the sovereign authority of Zeus. It is the tyranny of brute force; precisely what Prometheus was trying to bring to an end when he at first sided with Zeus in order to overthrow Chronos — the Lord of Time — whose absolute identification with Fate was even more oppressive.

Prometheus is bound by chains to a rock in the Caucasus Mountains, where the eagle of Zeus keeps tearing at, and feeding on, his liver, which regrows every night so that the titanic trickster can endure the same torture again the next day. The archaic Greeks used the glossy black liver by candlelight for fortune telling or seeing the future, akin to the crystal ball gazing of other psychics. So, this is a symbol of Zeus attempting to see what Prometheus already sees and knows. Zeus also keeps sending Hermes as an emissary to Prometheus in order to try to convince him to give up the secret. This is interesting because

Hermes is supposedly the trickster of the Olympian pantheon, but when Prometheus is bound, Hermes acts as a dutiful representative of the authority of Zeus. Those Hermetic mystics who like to see Hermes as a trickster would do well to remember this, and to recognize that Prometheus is the original trickster of the West.

While Prometheus is bound, he is visited by Io, a princess who Zeus lusted after and who, when she refused to give in to him for fear of what Hera (the wife of Zeus) would do to her out of jealous rage, was turned into a cow by Zeus. Despite his own horrendous suffering, Prometheus is able to empathize with Io and to console her, with their conversations serving to remind us of what a sadist Zeus is and how he visits the most horrendous misfortunes even on defenseless women who are as innocent as Io. This scene is also important because it is another point at which the myth of Prometheus connects back to a probable Iranian inspiration, or at least an Iranian parallel. The *Gathas* of Zarathustra (Zoroaster), his philosophical hymns, begin with a scene of "the cow" pleading, in a feminine voice, for a just protector from the wrath of the Daevas (the gods) and being answered by the "Titan of Wisdom" (Ahura Mazda), who appoints Zarathustra as her protector and the prophet tasked with enlightening mankind.

Prometheus reassures Io that Zeus will eventually be overthrown. What he refuses to reveal to Zeus, despite the torture at the hands of the eagle or the inquisitorial questioning by Hermes, is that Thetis is among the women that Zeus will rape in the future, serial rapist that he is. This would make Zeus the father of Achilles, the infamous hero or anti-hero of the Trojan War. As memorialized in Homer's *Iliad*, Achilles is the son of Thetis by the human father Peleus. This is not how it was supposed to be. Zeus somehow found out what Prometheus was refusing to tell him, and he refrained from raping Thetis so that Achilles would not be born as a "hero" in the true sense of being a hybrid or demi-god. Had he been born as such, he would have been destined to overthrow Zeus.

We can see this from the character that Achilles displays in the *Iliad*: in his prideful refusal to bow to Agamemnon, whom he considers a capriciously unjust king and commander, and in his relentless rage and wrathful persistence in disobedience, Achilles is the first figure in Greek literature or poetry to demonstrate a profound questioning of hitherto unquestioned norms that unconsciously equate the fact of the matter of how things are with how they ought to be. Before Achilles, the social order was not conceived of as separate from the natural order and this state of affairs, unconsciously governed by ancestral custom, was assumed to be a just expression of the divine will and the allotted fate of mankind. Achilles calls all of this into question, framing his perceived injustice in terms of a projected vision of an ideal order that would be more just than the world as it is. Moreover, he is willing to face the wrath of the gods and to let his own men be slaughtered by digging his heels in to pridefully stand against this injustice, and to stand for his sovereign individuality, until it sets an example that might inspire others to join this lonely insurrection. It makes perfect sense that this is the soul that Prometheus foresees as the type of person who would and could overthrow Zeus, that is, if he were to have been born as a demi-god with the abilities to do so. Still, what this part of the myth tells us is that, in principle, Zeus can and should be overthrown. This is something that we should hope for and aim to achieve.

The flames of this hope are fanned by the fact that Prometheus is eventually freed from his torment. In the course of his own heroic adventures, the strongman of unmatched might, Hercules (Herakles), happens upon Prometheus in the Caucasus Mountains. The location is not insignificant insofar as the forethought of Prometheus is connected to the thinking ahead that is demanded of people who live in parts of the world with long winters. This seasonal preparation, among the original Caucasians and the various Indo-Europeans (Aryans) who descended from them, has a lot to do with the predominance of *techne* and eventually of technological science among these peoples.

One does not find this among natives of parts of the world that lack seasons. According to some versions, Prometheus was specifically chained to the peak of Mt. Elbrus, after which the Iranians (Aryans) later named the Alborz Mountain Range once they migrated from the Caucasus to the land that they named "Iran" after themselves.

The Iranian connection is very important here because the Ossetians of Georgia, who are the last remnant of the Scythian branch of northern Iranians, have preserved a 3,000-year-old myth of a fire-bringing titan who teaches men to forge metal swords and leads them in a rebellion against God. He is punished by being bound on a peak in the Caucasus and tortured by the eagle of this God, who eats the titan's liver every day, only for it to grow back every night. In the Ossetian (Iranian) parts of the Caucasus, this titan is still referred to as *Amirani* or "I am Aryan," with the word "Aryan" (*Irani*) meaning "noble." More to the point is the fact that in the Amirani myth, the eagle of Zeus is eventually shot through by the arrows of a hero called Batraz, whom the Greeks referred to as "the Scythian Hercules." In the eastern Iranian tradition, this "Scythian Hercules" comes to be known as Rostamé Sakzi (Rostam the Scythian). With origins in the Mithraic religion of pre-Zoroastrian Iran, he is the single most important hero of the Persian national epic, the *Shahnameh* of Ferdowsi. To this day, in Georgia, there is a folk tradition of destroying eagles' nests to honor Amirani's defiance of an unjust God. Greek authors would also sometimes use the phrase "the Scythian peaks" when referring to where Prometheus was bound in the Caucasus. Thus, Hercules breaking Prometheus free from his shackles and hunting dead the eagle of Zeus seems, in an older, Scythian version of the Prometheus myth, to have been one of the heroic trials of Rostam.

The Prometheus myth as a whole appears to be a hybridization of the Amirani myth of Iranian Scythia with the Sumerian myth of Enki, which was adopted into the Iranian world when the Persian Empire incorporated Mesopotamia and even turned Babylon into the capital district of Imperial Iran. Hesiod, who first tells us the story (from a hostile Olympian Greek perspective) is from Anatolia, which comes under Iranian rule a little earlier than the Persian conquest and colonization of the eastern parts of Greece. Then, the version of Aeschylus, which frames Prometheus as the first hero of the first tragedy ever written in the West, is composed in the wake of the Persian integration of Ionia, the intellectual and cultural bastion of Greece, into Imperial Iran. Aeschylus himself served as a soldier in the Persian Wars, and yet he was able to portray his enemy sympathetically in his tragedy titled *The Persians*. Aeschylus even draws somewhat of a parallel between his portrayal of Xerxes, with his hubris, and his portrayal of Prometheus.

It is not at all incidental that the author of the first tragic trilogy in history not only made Prometheus the hero of this trilogy, but also introduced divergent perspectives and a theory of mind into performative art. He invented the stage play with multiple actors, as viewed by an audience in an amphitheater (where divergent perspectives on the play are literally introduced by the architectural structure as well). Prior to Aeschylus, such as when Hesiod performed his traditionalist pieces, like the *Theogony*, there was only a single bard, perhaps backed up by a chorus. It is Aeschylus who introduces multiple actors, with different perspectives that the audience is invited to identify with and flip between, such as the multiple perspectives offered by the characters of Prometheus, Kratos, Hermes, Zeus, Io, Oceanus, Hercules, and others in the trilogy of *Prometheus the Fire Bringer*, *Prometheus Bound*, and *Prometheus Unbound*.

Later authors throughout the Hellenistic period adopted and adapted the story of Prometheus, from Apollodorus of Athens (180–120 BC) to Zosimos of Panopolis (flourished 300 AD). The latter wrote the first surviving treatises on alchemy, and he associated Prometheus, as a patron spirit of alchemy, with the teachings of Zoroaster (Zarathustra). The full breadth and depth of the influence of Prometheus on the nascent scientific culture and technological revolution of the Hellenistic world cannot be known, since 90% of the scientific and literary treatises were lost when Christian mobs attacked and burned institutions such as the Library of Alexandria. It is only in the early modern period that the Prometheus myth re-emerges, together with technological science, as a symbol of human self-determination, exploration, and innovation.

Many of the great romantic writers of the modern age saw Prometheus as a champion of humanity, adopting his heroic defiance of Zeus and his gift of *techne* to mankind as a symbol with which to oppose theocratic and monarchical tyranny and to promote intrepid scientific exploration and technological industriousness. Johann Wolfgang von Goethe, who is better known for his portrayal of *Faust* and for contributing to the eventual framing of Western Civilization as the "Faustian World" by Oswald Spengler, actually admitted that amidst his own dark night of the soul he accepted Prometheus as his personal god and savior. In addition to Goethe's "Prometheus" poem (1774), there is also one by Lord Byron (1816), which emphasizes how Prometheus was unjustly punished for his compassionate beneficence toward Man, and how he is willing to endure a fate worse than death, a seemingly interminable hell, in steadfast defiance of "the Thunderer" and the will of "inexorable Heaven."

Lord Byron's close friend Percy Shelley wrote the most epic exploration of the titanic tragedy in his four-act lyrical drama *Prometheus Unbound* (1820). Shelley's portrayal of Prometheus is the most overtly Satanic. He makes it clear enough that Prometheus is none other than Lucifer, and he also incorporates the legend of the destruction of Atlantis while identifying Atlantis with the biblical pre-flood civilization sired by the Fallen Angels and destroyed by God because God wants to keep humanity ignorant and enslaved. The most famous of the modern adaptations of the Prometheus myth is, however, that penned by his wife, Mary Shelley, on a dark and stormy night on Lake Geneva with Percy and Lord Byron. *Frankenstein; or, The Modern Prometheus* (1818) went on to deeply influence many other

Promethean works of science fiction, up to and including Sir Ridley Scott's *Prometheus* (2012) and *Alien Covenant* (2017).

It was not lost on me that Scott portrayed the albino Engineers in the *Prometheus* film and its sequel as having the same whiteness as the whale in *Moby Dick*, the whiteness of the whale that I saw suspended in the night sky over doomed Atlantis. This passage from Melville's forty-second chapter, on "The Whiteness of the Whale," strikes me as uncannily relevant to that terrible thing that I glimpsed as a child in the Hall of Ocean Life at the Museum of Natural History:

> But not yet have we solved the incantation of this whiteness, and learned why it appeals with such power to the soul; and more strange and far more portentous — why, as we have seen, it is at once the most meaning symbol of spiritual things, nay, the very veil of the Christian's Deity; and yet should be as it is, the intensifying agent in things the most appalling to mankind.
>
> Is it that by its indefiniteness it shadows forth the heartless voids and immensities of the universe, and thus stabs us from behind with the thought of annihilation, when beholding the white depths of the milky way? Or is it, that as in essence whiteness is not so much a color as the visible absence of color; and at the same time the concrete of all colors; is it for these reasons that there is such a dumb blankness, full of meaning, in a wide landscape of snows — a colorless, all-color of atheism from which we shrink?

CHAPTER 3

THE FLAG OF AHAB

When *Prometheus and Atlas* won the book award at the 2016 Parapsychological Association conference, it already featured, on its dust jacket, the review by Jeffrey Mishlove. As the only person in the United States to hold a PhD in Parapsychology from a prominent university, UC Berkely, and as the single person who had done most to popularize Parapsychology through his original *Thinking Allowed* television series, where he interviewed tens of leading lights in the field after having read their books and studied their theories, Mishlove had this to say about my magnum opus:

> *Prometheus and Atlas* is the most brilliant treatise relating to parapsychological material that I have ever encountered... it is also a very serious exploration of depth psychology and mythology. Jorjani's emphasis on what he terms "the spectral" affords us an opportunity to expand some of our existing models concerning psi. ...Jorjani has written the definitive book regarding the proper place of psi phenomena in the history of philosophical ideas... However, *Prometheus and Atlas* takes the argument much further and demonstrates that parapsychology and psi phenomena can be viewed, not only within the history of philosophy, but in the larger context of cultural history itself. Jorjani examines the mechanistic worldview [that] dominates science and has led to the marginalization of parapsychology (as well as many other cultural imbalances). The range of scholarship required to make this argument is, in my estimation, nothing short of awesome. I

> don't think any other writer comes even close to tying things together the way Jorjani has done. The experience of reading it is rather like gazing out at a brilliant starry sky, with many interrelated constellations, stars, and planets. Each is beautiful and unique and, together, one senses a whole cosmos.

Jeffrey Kripal also wrote a review of *Prometheus and Atlas*. As it turned out, he was an invited speaker at the 2016 Parapsychological Association conference, where *The Super Natural*, the book that he co-authored with Whitley Strieber, competed with, and lost to, *Prometheus and Atlas* for the book award. We had dinner together. I vividly recall Kripal looking down at the discarded crusts of my pizza slices with a very disturbed look on his face. Then he covered them with his napkin, as if he were throwing a sheet over a corpse. He said, by way of apology, "They look like mangled bodies!" As I recall, he delivered his invited lecture on the designated night, but did not stay for the awards ceremony. It would probably have been awkward for him to have heard his review read out before I approached the podium to accept the book award:

> Jason Jorjani's *Prometheus and Atlas* is what profound philosophical writing used to be but has long refused to be: visionary in its method and content, sweeping in its scope, literally mythical, and, above all, positive. That is a gross understatement, though. His notions of the paranormal as normal, of a coming spectral revolution, of a future spectral technology, and of a still unrealized but very real superhuman potential come together to form a coherent but still emerging worldview that is neither modern nor postmodern but something other and more.

The most insightful, and prophetic, review of *Prometheus and Atlas* was neither the one penned by Mishlove nor that of Kripal. Rather, it was the review written by James O'Meara for Counter-Currents. His review concludes by comparing the book to *Moby Dick* and describing yours truly as the standard-bearer of Captain Ahab. Toward the end of his lengthy piece, James O'Meara asks:

> Is not Melville's novel America's spectral epic? ... Is not Ahab our Prometheus with his never healed wound, our Atlas with his obsessive sea charts tracking the great White Whale around the globe, ultimately our Lucifer? And does he not unite a cosmopolitan crew behind his Faustian quest? And does the last sight of the Pequod conjure up the fraternal statues with which Professor Jorjani started his — and our — voyage?

Then O'Meara continues by quoting a passage from the last part of Melville's epic:

> A *sky-hawk* that tauntingly had followed the main-truck downwards from *its natural home among the stars, pecking at the flag, and incommoding Tashtego* there; this bird now chanced to intercept its broad fluttering wing between *the hammer* and the wood; and simultaneously feeling that ethereal thrill, the submerged savage beneath, in his depth-gasp, kept his hammer frozen there; and so *the bird of heaven, with archangelic shrieks, and his imperial beak thrust upwards, and his whole captive form folded in the flag of Ahab, went down with his ship, which, like Satan, would not sink to hell till she had dragged a living part of heaven along with her, and helmeted herself with it.* Now *small fowls flew screaming* over the yet yawning gulf; a *sullen white surf* beat against its steep sides; then all collapsed, and the great shroud of the sea rolled on *as it rolled five thousand years ago.*

O'Meara ends with the following reflection on this quote, and on my relationship with Ahab: "...*Prometheus and Atlas* is our nonfiction *Moby Dick*, Titanic in its scope and intention, stuffed with encyclopedic lore, cosmopolitan and yet essentially American, and Professor Jorjani is our 'pagan harpooner' folded in the flag of Ahab." In the end it was Jeffrey Kripal and Jeffrey Mishlove who, between the two of them, did the most to fold me in the flag of Ahab.

In July of 2018, I visited Jeffrey Kripal at his home in Houston, Texas. I had actually been staying with Shahin Nezhad, the leader of the Iranian Renaissance, who also lives in Houston, and so I decided to use that visit with Shahin and his wife Artemis to catch up with Kripal as well and fill him in on the true story behind my public scandal. At that point, I had already been defamed as a genocidal Neo-Nazi in the pages of *The New York Times, Newsweek, The Intercept*, and *Jacobin*, on *NBC*, as well as numerous other mainstream media outlets. Meanwhile, Persian language media had defamed me as a Zionist agent of the Mossad on account of my attempt to broker an alliance between the faction around then Israeli Defense Minister Avigdor Lieberman and Iranian nationalists—including those operating discretely *within* the power structure of the Islamic Republic.

I was really disturbed when I walked into Kripal's home, because the walls were covered in various paintings of jellyfish. He said that his daughter had made them. I explained to him that it was an unsettling synchronicity, considering the fact that the intelligence agency principally involved in my defamation was named Jellyfish. I told Kripal how, a few months after *Prometheus and Atlas* was published in February of 2016, I was approached by the London-based man who I referred to as "Frederick Boulder" in *Uber Man.* He said that the salvaged intelligence directorate of Blackwater, now rebranded as "Jellyfish" and nominally run by Michael Bagley in Washington, DC, was at his disposal. "Boulder" made a concrete offer to put me in touch with Bagley so that the latter could assist the Iranian Renaissance, which I had just begun working with, in their efforts to bombard people inside of Iran with anti-Islamic Republic propaganda. As I related to Kripal, I took Boulder up on this, and Bagley was, before long coordinating with the Iranian Renaissance leadership, through me, to use a satellite broadcast facility based in Croatia to beam content into Iran geared toward a resurgence of pre-Islamic Persian culture.

This was, however, only Boulder's hook to involve me in a number of esoteric projects. These ranged from cloning and genetic experimentation with recovered remains of Nordic supermen entombed at various megalithic sites, to an attempt to enlist the British Society for Psychical Research into developing an X-Men-style manor home where gifted people would have their psi ability trained, to retrofitting the Nazi "Bell" design to contemporary technological standards. I set up a meeting between Boulder and John Poynton, the head of the British SPR, who, to his credit, flatly refused to get involved in the psi project. As for the "Bell" retrofitting, I took a former NASA Jet Propulsion Laboratory scientist to a meeting that I set up for us with Jacques Vallée, in his guise both as a UFO researcher and a Silicon Valley venture capitalist, at the Fairmont Hotel in San Francisco, where the engineer pitched the mercury-thorium reactor with a view to potential investor funding. As for the first of the aforementioned projects, the one involving genetic experimentation, and potential hybridization, using the genetic material recovered from the remains of excavated "Daevas," fortunately, I decided against sharing that with a tech billionaire who was based in Newport Beach, where Boulder's people supposedly also had a "stem cell clinic" acting as a front for such an operation. I have laid out all of this in much more detail in the second chapter of *Uber Man*, titled "Riding Satan's Ass," which is entirely non-fiction. The point of recapping it here is simply to say that I outlined all of this for Kripal, in his living room in July of 2018, so that he could understand the context of the defamation that had taken place almost a year earlier.

As part of this panoply of occult proposals, and much more concrete (but equally secret) plans for staging an Iranian Renaissance coup in Tehran (the first stage of which was eventually attempted, and failed, in the winter of 2017–2018), I was tasked with integrating the Arktos publishing house, Red Ice Radio and Television, and the National Policy Institute think tank into a single corporate entity, namely the Alt-Right Corporation, which was supposed to consolidate control over the then extremely chaotic and fractious "movement" (if it could even be called that), which was only loosely branded with the umbrella term "Alt-Right." I was promised a capital investment that would establish me as the CEO of this corporate entity, and thus by extension, a kind of corporatist man-in-the-shadows type leader of the Alt-Right and the European New Right that we planned to merge into it, including through the merger of Arktos and Red Ice (both run by Swedes) with the American-based NPI. My aim as CEO would then be to make the movement cohesive and organized enough to redirect its trajectory away from White Nationalism, European Ethnocentrism, and any other race-based politics, towards an implicitly cosmopolitan discourse of global "Indo-European civilizational unity."

Here my position within the innermost leadership circle of the Iranian Renaissance would be key, building a bridge between those who wanted to save the West from Muslim mass migration and those who wanted to restore the "Aryan" (simply the ancient form of the word "Iranian") culture of pre-Islamic Iran by carrying out, not just a political, but also a cultural revolution against the theocratic Muslim regime in power in Tehran. Bringing in Russia, India, and even the Buddhist countries of Eastern Asia, with Japan as their hub, was envisioned as an alternative to the isolationist worldview of American and European nationalists, and, for that matter, of equally racist Iranian fascists. How far from anything "Nazi" this vision was, is highlighted by the fact that, as part of this project, I had dealings with at least four different agents of the Mossad in a bid to secure the support of a pro-Persian faction within the State of Israel for the kind of change in Iran that would be needed to turn Iran from an Islamic Republic into a hub for a global Indo-European superstate stretching from California and Cascadia to Siberia and Japan. I even coined a discourse of "Iranian Zionism" for the sake of achieving this end, branding Iranians as history's first Zionists by arguing that the "Aryan" Achaemenid elite invented Zionism.

Once the promised funding was to come through, I was supposed to open a channel to Donald Trump in the White House via Steve Bannon, an avid reader of Arktos books. Richard Spencer was given to understand that I would be on point with this, not him. The Iranian Renaissance leadership, for their part, also wanted this channel and understood that I would employ it for their benefit as well, to influence Iran policy, as part of the over-arching "Indo-European World Order" project. My second book, *World State of Emergency*, published at the height of these dealings in the summer of 2017, was framed in a way that aimed to function as a policy proposal for this project and, frankly, to propagandize for it to all parties involved. That is especially true of the last third of the book. Unlike the first third of the text, which does develop an original philosophical concept in the context of a serious analysis of ideas, such as the nature of state sovereignty, the incoherence of democracy and universal human rights, and the middle section, which adequately conveys the convergent dangers of emergent technologies as a global threat, the last third of *World State of Emergency* is essentially the product of an intelligence operation gone wrong. An operation which, I realized very late in the game, had me and my career as its target from the beginning.

This is what I was trying to get across to Jeffrey Kripal in his living room in July of 2018, when I was still involved with the Iranian Renaissance but had left the Alt-Right. As I explain in detail in *Uber Man*, I later discovered (via someone in Mossad) that Boulder was an agent of British Intelligence. I was also told that "Hope not Hate," the London-based Antifa group that sent Patrick Hermansson to surreptitiously record me under the alias of "Erik Hellberg" (a supposed right-wing youth vouched for by those who invited me to the London Forum), is also a front for British Intelligence. Boulder was MI6. Hope not Hate may have been an MI5 operation at the time, but since opening a foreign branch in the USA it might have migrated into MI6 as well. In any case, Boulder set up my talk at the London Forum, and then refused to attend the behind-closed-doors meeting himself, claiming that a certain individual, who my Iranian Renaissance associates knew to be an agent of Scotland Yard, told him that the event was unsafe because it had been penetrated by Antifa. It is at that meeting that Patrick Hermansson first set his sights on me, before later setting me up at Jack Demsey's in Manhattan. Meanwhile, in all of the months between January, when the Alt-Right Corporation was formed on the promise of capital investment that would be imminently injected by Boulder's group through me, I was given repeated excuses for why the funding was being delayed, for a month, and then another, and another.

I would have called bullshit on the whole thing and resigned from the Alt-Right much earlier (early enough not to have been defamed with a spliced secret recording of me), had it not been for the fact that, at one point, Boulder volunteered to compensate for the missing funding by promising me a commission on a nearly one-billion dollar project to reconstruct the Venezuelan national oil industry ahead of a coup against the Maduro government that his people intended to carry out there (he told me this months before the first protests began in the failed coup attempt in Venezuela in 2017). Shahin Nezhad, the leader of the Iranian Renaissance, whose day job is working as a top-notch petroleum engineer, put this proposal in front of the head of Occidental Petroleum, who declined it only because the company claimed not to have the capabilities to carry it out successfully. Again, this is discussed in more detail in Chapter 2 of *Uber Man*. There, I also point out that the blackness of the water in Blackwater, of which Jellyfish was the salvaged intelligence directorate, refers to the oil of offshore oil platforms, and that what few people know is that the first incarnation of what became Blackwater and then Jellyfish was a certain "g3i Group" for security and intelligence with a focus on these rigs located in lawless international waters.

Anyway, I explained all of this to Kripal and told him that I had come to believe that Boulder and his group had targeted me, from the beginning, for what (I have since learned) intelligence officials call an "image cheapening" operation. Kripal's response, in the privacy of his living room, and of his upstairs office, decorated with items from the *X-Men* franchise that he is so enamored with, was to express appreciation for my courage. He understood that I had been willing to get my hands very dirty with the ultimately noble intention of redirecting the Alt-Right *away* from racism and nationalism, while at the same time freeing the Iranian people from repressive Muslim theocracy in a way that turns Iran into the hub of a wider *cosmopolitan* power structure (albeit compellingly branded as an "Indo-European World Order"), akin to the progressive and humanistic Achaemenid Empire, rather than some conservative and protectionist Neo-Zoroastrian (or Neo-Sassanid) fascist regime (which is what a lot of Iranians and some of my former colleagues in the Iranian Renaissance want to see replace the Islamic Republic). Frankly, Kripal said, "You're much more courageous than me," and admitted that he would never have the guts to do something like what I had done, not because it was ethically wrong, but because he would be concerned for the comfort of his family and the security of the academic career that affords him the ability to care for them.

Kripal then agreed to write me a new, revised letter of recommendation for a round of applications to academic job openings that my attorney encouraged me to submit at least so as to secure the expected rejection letters as evidence of how I had been rendered unemployable on account of my defamation. To submit these letters with some measure of good faith, and at least a little hope that one of them might be accepted, I was waiting for Kripal's letter. Had he not agreed to write me that revised letter, offsetting the possible lack of support from other former recommenders cowered by the defamatory claims being made about me in the mainstream media at the time, I would have sought out other letters, which though of less value, would have completed the applications for submission.

On July 26, Kripal wrote: "I am willing to do this… I believe the academy should be the home of many viewpoints, not one. Let me give this a whirl, send it to you, and get your feedback. I want to make sure I am accurate and fair." Then, a month later, coming up against application deadlines he wrote: "I have been making my way through *Novel Folklore*, which is rich and complex… I am also well aware that you need an updated letter from me. …I want to do this for you." Finally, on October 21 of 2018, after a number of the academic job application deadlines (of which he had been made aware) had passed, Kripal wrote me the following: "I decided there was no real way I was ever going to understand what happened to you, and where I sit, or do not sit, with it all." *This* is what he chose to put on the record, in an email, as compared to what he volunteered to me in the privacy of his own home. I was so incensed at having been strung along for several months only to get this response that I did not even bother to submit the applications to those few jobs with submission deadlines that had not yet passed. I shared what happened with Jeffrey Mishlove, who, at the time, was quite displeased with Kripal's behavior in this affair. As it turned out, Mishlove would eventually wind up doing *far* worse himself—and he would be rewarded for it, by Kripal.

The date was October 1, 2020, just a little over two years later. In the several months since the founding of the Prometheist Movement on the fourth of July of that year, and ahead of the subsequent release of *Prometheism* in September, Mishlove and I had recorded several programs together about the book. Despite my defamation, I remained the most popular and widely demanded guest of *New Thinking Allowed*, a program that I principally inspired and encouraged Mishlove to create at the time that I met him back in 2015, when he was a businessman working in real estate (who had left the original *Thinking Allowed* twenty years behind him). Two of the three programs we recorded together had already been released. A third was cued up to be released soon, and we were in regular email communication. Jeff and I would also occasionally speak on the phone. That was the situation, at least on my end, when, out of the blue, on the first of October, I was informed that Mishlove had just aired an attack on me, personally, and on Prometheism as a movement, in the form of a monologue on the *New Thinking Allowed* channel. The piece had been pre-recorded before our last email communication, a day earlier, but Mishlove had mentioned nothing about his having recorded it, or his plan to release it the next day, in the course of that correspondence.

In the monologue, titled "Further Reflections on my friend Jason Reza Jorjani," Mishlove describes me as a "warmonger." He explicitly says that no one should follow me, and that my writings should be read only so that my ideas can be critically opposed. In the course of making these remarks, he conflates Prometheism with his misunderstandings of certain statements in *World State of Emergency*, a book that he had not taken the care to read until then (several years after I gave him multiple copies of it). This, despite the fact that the geopolitical vision of *World State of Emergency* is very different from that of *Prometheism*, and had already been abandoned by the time that I launched the Prometheist Movement, which is the real target of his monologue. Some direct quotes from his monologue are in order here:

> I am now left with the impression that my dear friend is a warmonger. I think it's a fair assessment to say at this point that Jason believes we've already entered the Third World War and that our only hope of victory at this point is to finish it off quickly, like in the next thirty years, to use the nuclear armaments of the United States and Russia and other Western nations to pretty much completely annihilate the Chinese and the Islamic World, and to establish Indo-European hegemony over the entire planet. He's arguing for that.
>
> He suggests, I believe, that we need a leader of the Western World, somebody who is strong enough to launch a nuclear war... He feels that such a scenario would be preferable to other alternatives. Preferable to a World State dominated by the Chinese or dominated by the Islamic World.
>
> … Another factor that I don't think Jason has begun to take into account is the role of commerce. The way in which both technology *and* commerce are creating a *global culture*. It's transactional, but it's a relatively peaceful culture. It may well be that we've reached a point where commerce trumps religion. Commerce trumps ethos — or *commerce is an ethos*. Well, I hate to even use the word 'trump' in this context, because that just raises another terrible specter.
>
> …I think being a warmonger… always suggests the risk that you might prevail. You might actually start a war. I think that Jason, who has a big following on the *New Thinking Allowed* channel, wishes to start a war.

> … His thinking is important to be understood, and recognized, *and countered.* … What I say is listen to Jason. *Don't follow Jason* but listen to him and address the concerns that he is raising.

Later, Mishlove would decide that his viewers shouldn't even listen to me, let alone follow me—*because he unlisted all of the 37 video interviews that we recorded together over the course of five years*, but we will come to that. Let me not get ahead of myself. Before launching into a commentary on Mishlove's monologue, it must be noted that he also repeatedly said that he loves me in the course of it. But such statements, when taken together with his maniacal laughter, only raise the question of whether he is suffering from some kind of deep cognitive dissonance, unless the apparent contradiction is to be explained by interpreting the whole piece as terribly condescending, patronizing, and paternalistic in a way that deeply disrespects me while taking aim at the movement that I had just founded.

"Warmonger" is a derogatory epithet. If Mishlove had said "Jason has a militaristic mindset," or "my friend is very aggressive in his view of war," or something of the sort, he would have made true statements while also distancing himself from my geopolitical philosophy. Even if he had said, "Jason is advocating violence," that would have been true. Yes, as a revolutionary, I advocate violent rebellion. In the first paragraph of "The Prometheist Manifesto" and the book *Prometheism*, I make clear that the "war" I am declaring is a *revolutionary* war—a long-term struggle against the tyranny of an elite of actual warmongers and social engineers who rule over humanity like sadistic archons.

David is not a "warmonger." Goliath is the "warmonger." I had already made it clear to anyone who paid attention to the message of Prometheism that the Prometheist Movement will only ever be David, never Goliath. Now, the proposal for an Indo-European World Order in *World State of Emergency* (2017) was a kind of Goliath, but I had clearly rejected that vision by the time I founded the Prometheist Movement. The geopolitics of *Prometheism* (2020), which reaches back to my embryonic political philosophy in *Prometheus and Atlas* (2016), is radically different from that and at odds with it. Even the geopolitics of *Iranian Leviathan* (2019) already rejected the Indo-European World Order proposal of *World State of Emergency*, which, as I explained above, was developed as part of an intelligence operation.

"Warmonger" means someone who wants to start a war because he enjoys war for its own sake. I am certainly *not* a warmonger. In fact, I went to great lengths, and endured public chastisement (as an "Iranian Zionist" in Persian-language media) with attacks from every direction, in order to stop a war between Israel and Iran by trying to make peace between two key factions within the Israeli and Iranian power structures. I was publicly and vehemently opposed to the US-led wars in both Afghanistan (2001) and Iraq (2003), as well as the NATO bombing of Syria, and I consistently stood against American or allied military intervention as a means to effect regime change in Iran.

By contrast, Jeffrey Mishlove, who hypocritically claims to be "a pacifist," was an enthusiastic supporter of, and donor to, the presidential campaigns of Barack Obama and Hillary Clinton. Obama continued the unjustified wars in Iraq and Afghanistan, bombed Syria, and attempted regime changes in Egypt and Libya that could also have led to war and that, in the case of Libya, did result in bloody and ongoing civil strife in a country that, under Muammar Ghaddafi, had enjoyed relative prosperity and security. For her part, as a Senator, Hillary Clinton voted for the war in Iraq in 2003, although Iraq had nothing to do with 9/11 and Saddam had no weapons of mass destruction. That war cost the lives of 200,000 Iraqi civilians in order to replace the secular republic of Saddam Hussein with a backwards and at least equally repressive Islamic theocracy. As Secretary of State for Obama, and as a presidential candidate, Hillary Clinton was in favor of military intervention in Syria and Libya. Worst of all, she kept beating the drums for going to war against Iran in alignment with, and in the interests of, Saudi Arabia and the other Arab oil emirates in the Persian Gulf.

It is true that, after my defamation, Mishlove helped to raise some funding for me (because I had been rendered unemployable and had very significant legal expenses). I might add that Mishlove is a very wealthy man, who lives in a palatial home (which makes his attack on me, while I was destitute, a rather cheap thing). Whatever Mishlove himself had contributed to me was far less than his campaign contributions to Obama and Clinton, who are *actual* war criminals.

Now let us construct something logical out of his logically inconsistent claims that "commerce trumps ethos" and also that "commerce *is* an ethos." What Mishlove means to say is that commerce is an ethos that trumps every other ethos, including the ethos of any and all religions of every culture on the planet. What would it even mean for commerce to be an ethos? The Greek word *ethos* means the fabric or fiber of a person's character as shaped by certain ideals and principles, on the basis of one or another philosophical or religious standpoint—often associated with one or another culture, but potentially cosmopolitan or universalist. Commerce is nothing other than the "transactional" nature of business, in which everything and (since slavery, including wage slavery, and prostitution are also "commerce") every*one* is for sale at *some* price.

For commerce to be one's ethos is an incredibly perverse statement wherein the person in question is admitting that *for him* there are no values above or beyond, or beneath (deeper than) the potentially global sphere of transactional business. To then take the further step, as Mishlove does, of claiming that the "commerce ethos" now legitimately trumps any and every other ethos essentially amounts to a will to capture everything that any culture or group holds to be sacred, and that the members of that community are willing to fight and die for, within the calculative net or mesh of global business transactions. That is why he supposes (wrongly) that it will yield a "peaceful" world—a world wherein everyone has a price, and nothing is *worth* dying for.

Call me a romantic, but I would sooner see my worst enemies — Chinese Confucianists and the Sunni Caliphate — rule large parts of the planet than to live in a world pacified by such "transactions" wherein every soul is for sale and every great cause has been sold out. When Mishlove made *this* statement, I suddenly realized, to my horror, that I have more in common with some of the worst enemies of the Promethean ethos that I embrace than I do with the likes of him. What he went on to add about various other subjects only underlined that terrible realization.

On October 11, Mishlove came out with a second statement about me in the course of a live question and answer session. He said a number of things there that made clear the position (if it can even be called that) from which he levelled his attack on me. Mishlove begins by saying that, contrary to "a lot of… conspiracy theories," the Federal Reserve is a trustworthy institution run by people who "are conscientious" and "want to do good." "Conscientious" is also a word that he uses to describe the financial and political establishment as a whole, as well as most of the mainstream media: "I am generally in *favor* of the establishment. I *used* to be an anti-establishment person," and he laughs at himself as he says this, "back in the day when I was protesting the war in Vietnam." Let us just pause there for a moment to recall that, as a strong supporter of Hillary Clinton, Mishlove would not have protested the Vietnam War today, despite claiming to be a "pacifist" who believes that "war is evil," because the Iraq and Afghanistan wars, taken together, were worse American aggressions than Vietnam.

Mishlove does not want to see that the likes of Hillary Clinton and others in "the establishment" who start these wars to make money for private banking institutions, such as the so-called "Federal" Reserve, are the *same* exact types, at the RAND Corporation, Dow Chemical, and so forth, who dropped napalm on Vietnamese children. Henry Kissinger, the greatest war criminal in the history of the United States, has probably served as the closest advisor that Hillary Clinton has ever had. Mishlove continues, "But these days I tend to think that *most* people — not everybody, certainly — but most people who work in establishment organizations are conscientious. They're trying to do the right thing *most* of the time." Then, as if this was not bad enough, he gratuitously goes on to add, "So I trust the mainstream media. I trust *mostly* what I hear from the government. There are certainly exceptions, including one *very big* exception [President Trump], but in any case, I have faith in humanity as a whole."

One of the many things that the Mainstream Media and the government can be trusted about is that they are not lying to us on the subject of UFOs. They are just telling us what they know, whenever they come to know it. According to Mishlove, there has been no large-scale UFO cover-up by the United States government. There will be no UFO "Disclosure" because there is nothing hidden for the government to disclose to us:

> Bit by bit things are being disclosed, because bit by bit we're learning — and that's about it. I don't think there's going to be any huge disclosure coming… because I don't think that there are [any] people who have a full knowledge *at all.* I think there will be a gradual UFO disclosure *as we learn more.* I know there are many people who *suggest* that the government knows a lot more than it's saying. I'm not convinced that that's the case.

Then Mishlove expresses his "oneness with everything in the universe, and that includes all the UFOs and all of their occupants." On the authority of Darryl Anka, some new age medium, the "channeled" messages of which Mishlove says he doesn't see "any reason offhand not to take seriously," all of those coming here in UFOs must be beneficent enlightened beings from a civilization that is necessarily more ethical than ours because it is much older and thus more advanced than ours. After all, "we're a new civilization" with "a written history going back, you know, five, ten, fifteen thousand years at most." What about Atlantis? He was asked that during this same Q&A session. His answer. It is a "conspiracy theory." He doesn't give it more than "maybe ten percent" likelihood. How about "hidden UFO bases" that multiple

US government remote viewers have seen "on Mars or on the Moon or anywhere else"? Well, that's also a conspiracy theory. He gives it "maybe ten percent" as well. As for "all kinds of *other conspiracy theories*," he says in a dismissive tone, you know, things like the JFK assassination or 9/11 having been an inside job, "I'd maybe give it *five percent*," he concludes as he laughs mockingly.

In other words, extensive forensic investigations into the Kennedy Assassination and the controlled demolition of the Twin Towers on 9/11, which have been repeatedly conducted by tens of academically competent and scientifically trained researchers, are laughable "conspiracy theories" but there is no reason not to take the channeler, Daryl Anka, seriously when he claims that all of the UFO occupants are more enlightened and more ethical than we are. Forget the mass of evidence for horrendously abusive "alien" abductions, terrifying cattle mutilations, and worst of all, the manipulation of our large-scale belief systems for thousands of years, including to start huge wars—crusades and jihads—in the name of false "revelations" from these "aliens" posing as gods and angels.

No, all of that is "conspiracy theory." Just like Atlantis. Because if we had a civilization like Atlantis here tens of thousands of years ago, with technology so advanced that the culture was space-faring, then the demise of that civilization, let alone the evidence suggesting that it was somehow connected to a nuclear war on Mars, and to other nuclear exchanges on Earth, would put the lie to Mishlove's preposterously naïve belief in "enlightenment" qua moral betterment being linearly pegged to scientific and technological progress.

Mishlove conveniently forgets that all of the most scientifically advanced and technologically adept cultures in our own modern history, from the British Empire to Nazi Germany, were also the most brutally exploitative colonial powers to ever appear on the face of the Earth. Why would it be otherwise in space? *If* UFOs are even coming from outer space, which they are *not*. But the knowledge that they are from here, from hidden bases on Earth, the Moon, Mars, and other places in *this* solar system, and that they represent part of a human civilization that extends back *millions* of years, which has been war-torn and plagued by slave-driving tyranny for just as long, is among the secrets that the trustworthy US government couldn't possibly be hiding from us. The Mainstream Media wouldn't hide it either. They mean well, and they don't lie.

It is because Mishlove dismisses all narratives that question the position of the establishment and the Mainstream Media as "conspiracy theories," no matter how well researched and empirically substantiated these "theories" are, that he also grossly misrepresents my position on China in his two monologues of October 2020. In an April 27, 2020, blog post titled "The Chinese Virus and World War III," with specific reference to *World State of Emergency* as having been prescient, I warned that if the People's Republic of China did not admit that Covid-19 was manufactured as a Chinese military bioweapon at their Wuhan laboratory and apologize for its having "accidentally" leaked out of the lab, then it would have to be assumed that the engineered virus was deliberately released. At that point in the spring of 2020, I put the deadline for this admission at the moment when a potential second wave of Covid-19 was about to hit the Western world, which was being used to justify mandated vaccination with dangerously untested mRNA technology (which the Chinese, and the Russians for that matter, had no intention of using in their own conventional Covid vaccines). This second wave began in early September of 2020, when *Prometheism* was released. Meanwhile, more evidence was uncovered that Covid-19 is a chimera hybrid virus engineered by the Chinese regime, albeit with help from treasonous Western corporatists involved in gain-of-function research, not the least of whom was Covid Tsar Anthony Fauci himself.

In my April 27th blog post, against the backdrop of a broader geopolitical and civilizational context first laid out in *World State of Emergency*, I had argued that, in the absence of a Chinese admission to manufacturing the virus and a convincing explanation of how it was "accidentally" released, the onset of a second wave, and attendant forced vaccinations with an unsafe technology promoted by the same compromised elites who funded the work at Wuhan, would have to be considered a Chinese initiation of the Third World War by use of a Weapon of Mass Destruction. So, it should have come as no surprise that on September 4, 2020, I tweeted (on Twitter) and posted (on Facebook) that "China is an existential enemy of all Aryan civilizations (The West, Russia, Iran, India, and the Buddhists). We must join forces to wage a total war against the Chinese while we can still win it."

What I was advocating there was nothing different from one of the accepted US/NATO strategic doctrines during the Cold War with the Soviet Union. Had the Soviets used even a single WMD against the civilian population of the United States or Europe, a full-scale NATO nuclear strike against the Soviet Union would have been justified. Though this is not the *only* response that was considered, it was one accepted strategy based on the rather self-evident rationale that *if* the enemy is going to make a nuclear war necessary by striking with a WMD first, at whatever scale, the way to minimize casualties on one's own side is to maximize the second strike and leave the enemy with as little for a third strike as possible, thereby preventing protracted losses on *both* sides.

In fact, I even checked with a friend of mine who served at a very high level in the Pacific Command of the US Navy, who confirmed to me that because US military capability had been allowed to degrade so badly since the fall of the USSR in 1991, and since China had been allowed to emerge as a new rival military superpower, taking the place of the Soviet Union, it is now unfortunately the case that the only way we could still win a war with China would be to strike as hard and fast as possible. A full-scale war with China, which would be inevitable in the event that the truth about Covid-19 were admitted, is not a war that we could win if it were to stretch on for even one or two weeks. It would have to end within 24 to 48 hours, with most of their capability to strike back at us having been destroyed by then. Even still, we would lose millions of Americans. But, in a protracted war, it would be tens of millions and the United States would not survive as a functional political entity. The only caveat he had was to tell me that there are now other weapons besides nuclear weapons, equally destructive but more exotic and not radioactive, which the US Navy could use to deliver such a blow.

Also worthy of note, my mention of Russia as a potential ally with us against China was about a year and a half prior to the attempt to bring the Ukraine into NATO, which triggered Putin's military intervention. As you may recall from my interview to enter the Dalton School at age 11 in 1992, recounted in Chapter 2, I have always seen the Russians as potential partners in building a Promethean world order. That Russia was allowed to sink back into Orthodoxy under the leadership of a conservative like Vladimir Putin, and under the advisement of a Traditionalist like Alexander Dugin, is *entirely* the fault of the US-led NATO bloc that humiliated and raped a defeated Russia in the 1990s, instead of giving the Russians the bear hug that would have brought them securely into our orbit with an assurance of mutual respect and a restoration of their dignity (including a Marshall Plan for the recovery of their post-Soviet economy).

As I explained in *Uber Man*, my view is that we actually ought not to have ever tried to collapse the Soviet Union, but if that was going to be done, then America should have helped Russia stand back up on her feet, instead of trying to strangle her, in violation of the agreement with Gorbachev not to further expand NATO into the former Eastern bloc that we should have recognized as Russia's legitimate strategic sphere. Let alone the Ukraine, or Kievan Rus, which is no less than the civilizational fountainhead of Russia and has been socially re-engineered into a so-called "sovereign nation."

In any case, my point is that the pro-Biden liberals, like Mishlove, who are horrified by my statements about China, have fully backed Biden's march into a potential nuclear war with Russia, which we would have absolutely *no chance* of winning—as compared to a rapid engagement with China. Of course, even the latter is no longer an option on the table, because on account of the measures taken by US/NATO, including unprecedented measures to cut Russia and its partners out of the world economy, China and Russia are now in total lockstep so that, unlike back in 2020 when I made those statements, waging war against one of them would be to wage war against both. *That* is not a war that US/NATO could win. What I said back then I said because it was our last chance. At this point, living under a global Chinese hegemony is totally inevitable and the struggle against that will not be an international war; it will be a revolutionary war—a Promethean resistance struggle against a regressive worldwide collective tyranny that frames itself as a regime of "world peace" potentially wrapped in the flag of the United Nations. Well, my response to that is the flag of Ahab.

That brings me to another question that somebody asked Mishlove during the Q&A session on October 11 of 2020: "Is freedom more important than peace?" To which he responds with this gem that disregards the entire history of revolutionary wars and resistance movements in the name of liberty and liberation:

> Well, I think that freedom and peace go together. You know, it's usually in times of war when citizens give the government power for conscription and it's in times of war when the government propaganda machines try to curtail people's freedom to think even. So, I don't think that freedom is more important than peace, and I don't think it's a trade-off either. I think that if you want freedom, you also want peace.
>
> … Peace begets peace, war begets war, love begets love, hate begets hate, and that is true on the individual level and on the national level. So, if you want freedom, then I encourage you to work for peace.

Then Mishlove would have preferred that Europeans just peacefully lived under Nazi occupation? So, we shouldn't have gone to war against the Nazis. So, Charles de Gaulle wasn't the leader of a French freedom-fighting resistance. He was trying to curtail people's freedom by going to war against the Nazi occupiers and their puppet regime. We here in America should to this day be part of the British Empire, and those terrorists like George Washington who went to war against the British government also wanted to curtail people's freedom. To think that their revolutionary war was for the sake of liberty is just warmongering propaganda aiming to constrain people's freedom to think. That's why they baptized in blood and fire a constitutional order with the Bill of Rights at its core, enshrining liberties like a citizen's right to bear arms even against his own government should it become tyrannical.

Tyrannical how? By disregarding liberties such as freedom of speech, freedom of the press, freedom of assembly, protection against unlawful search and seizure—all of which, as of 2023, under the Biden administration, have now been almost entirely annulled by the farcical husk that remains of the US government—*with the approval of Mishlove,* who suffered from Trump derangement syndrome to the extent that he let his Rachel Maddow-watching wife ban two of his closest friends, both PhDs, from his home on account of their having been supporters of President Trump. When he did this, I should have seen his cancellation of me coming.

In early 2022, it was brought to my attention that all of my *New Thinking Allowed* video interviews had disappeared from YouTube. No search could retrieve them. Not on YouTube itself and not on Google or any other search engine. I still had a direct link to them in my playlists, so I was able to click through to them that way, only to discover that each and every one of them had been "unlisted." I wrote to Mishlove (for the first time since his October 2020 monologues) to ask him whether someone working for NTA, perhaps his new co-host, had done this without his knowledge. Mishlove wrote back, saying that he had done it himself, so as to prevent anyone else from finding my "Prometheism cult of personality" through these videos and being impressed enough to join the movement. He took it upon himself to do this despite the many trips I took flying from New York to Las

Vegas, and then later to Albuquerque, and the hundreds of hours I spent preparing for and recording those 37 programs with him—including at least an hour of tutoring him before each program, so that he would ask the right questions. Mishlove also did this despite my being the most popular guest on the show, which would not have existed but for my catalyzing its creation in 2015.

First of all, Prometheism bears no resemblance whatsoever to a cult of personality. I have a handful of administrators, each and every one of which would confirm that in the strongest terms, and who would also tell you that I am rubbed very much the wrong way by anything "cult of personality"-like that ever crops up from one or another misguided person who enters our orbit. I never promote such things, and if Prometheism were to ever devolve into a "cult," I would destroy it myself. Jiddu Krishnamurti was one of my heroes in my late teens and early twenties, and the example he set with the dissolution of the Order of the Star is never far from my mind or heart. He who has ears, let him hear.

Secondly, this move on Mishlove's part is as patronizing and paternalistic as his public attack on me (in which he repeatedly claims to "love" me). It is also hypocritical in light of his claim to have "faith in humanity as a whole." Apparently, Mishlove does not have enough faith in his viewers, who ought to represent a demographic way above the average of humanity in terms of their discernment, to make up their own minds about what I have to say. He feels that he needs to decide *for* them by removing the risk that they might hear and see something from me that compels them to dig further and then, ultimately, join the Prometheist Movement. This is exactly the logic behind the contemporary cancel culture on the Left.

In the same email exchange in which Mishlove admitted to having cancelled me himself, he said that I screwed myself out of $250,000. He claimed that prior to my refusal to come back onto *New Thinking Allowed* after his October 2020 monologues unless he apologized publicly, and prior to my going on to vote for Trump a second time in the November 2020 US presidential election, and my having called out the multi-faceted fraud perpetrated during that election to bring the totally corrupt and compromised Biden administration to power, Mishlove was considering making me a co-author for the essay on consciousness surviving bodily death that went on to win first prize in the Bigelow Institute for Consciousness Studies (BICS) essay competition for evidence of life beyond the brain. The grand prize was half a million dollars, which he claimed that he would have split with me if I had behaved after his monologues. Who served as the Bigelow-appointed judge responsible for awarding that $500K to Jeffrey Mishlove, despite his already being a multi-millionaire? None other than Jeffrey Kripal.

In what capacity was Kripal chosen by Bigelow to be the judge for the competition? Well, aside from his academic credentials and area of study, Kripal had recently become Chairman of the Board of Trustees at the Esalen Institute. Esalen is the cradle of the Human Potential Movement. It was founded in 1962 by Stanford graduates Michael Murphy and Dick Price at hot springs in Big Sur, California, overlooking the Pacific Ocean. Decades of research on our hidden potential and latent capacities, as demonstrated by the extraordinary abilities of certain humans throughout the centuries, yielded the bible of the Human Potential Movement, *The Future of the Body*, published by Michael Murphy in 1992. By then Esalen had become one of the wellsprings of the Counter Culture of the '60s and '70s, as well as the New Age movement of the '80s. The Esalen Institute had also developed a rather close relationship with certain more dynamic groups within the US military and intelligence community. Private meetings in the hot springs of Esalen, between American thinkers and their counterparts from the Eastern bloc, even played a key role in helping to mediate the end of the Cold War by 1991.

As Kotler and Wheal explain in *Stealing Fire*, at the core of the Human Potential Movement is the deliberate cultivation of STER, which means Selflessness, Timelessness, Effortlessness, and Richness.

These descriptors are meant to be purely phenomenological and are content-neutral. They claim that the "self" or voice in one's head as the source of suffering from "depression, anxiety, anger, jealousy, and other negative emotions." This is generated by the prefrontal cortex. Shutting it off for a while is technically referred to as "transient *hypofrontality*." One of Kotler and Wheal's characterizations of the benefit of Selflessness sounds an awful lot like the capacity to remain in a state of (induced) cognitive dissonance. Quoting Kegan's book *In Over Our Heads*, they write, "You start… constructing a world that is much more friendly to contradiction, to oppositeness, to being able to hold onto multiple systems of thinking… This means that the self is more about movement through different forms of consciousness than about defending and identifying with any one form." Is this really a way to "gain perspective" as per my concept of Destructive Departure in Worldview Warfare, or is it a way to shut off one's analytical discernment?

There are other dangers to ego death that are most un-Promethean. These include groupthink. Sri Rajneesh (aka "Osho"), Marshall Applewhite of Heaven's Gate, and Charles Manson are all examples of modern-day "pied pipers" or cult leaders who led their followers either to their deaths or to be responsible for the deaths of others. These are other possible outcomes of the same kind of replacement of the "I" with a hive mind that allows enhanced collaboration among Google programmer work groups or specially trained Navy SEAL teams to operate so effectively as a unit. Irrational collectivism can easily replace rational individualism under these conditions.

Transient hypofrontality also shuts off our ability to draw a distinction between the past and the future in a way that plunges us into "the deep now" or an indefinitely elongated present. In other words, Timelessness. Misattributing an ontological significance to this leads STER junkies to falsely believe that historical progress, and the need to forge a better future, are illusory or limited perspectives as compared to some putative truth of Eternity beyond the veil of *Maya*, wherein everything in the past and future is "really" happening at once or has already happened. Nothing could be further from the Promethean ethos of preparing for, and striving to build, the most ideal future.

"Effortlessness" refers to a "flow" state wherein six neurotransmitters spike in certain sequences. These are norepinephrine, dopamine, endorphins, serotonin, anandamide, and oxytocin. Each of them is among the most pleasurable chemicals that the brain produces, and in a flow state we gain exceptional access to many or all of them at once. In a flow state, there is tremendous motivation to do one or another thing, in a state of seemingly inexhaustible energy (for however long the flow lasts), and with the fluidity of things going without a hitch — in other words, being in masterful control on a nearly unconscious level. But Effortlessness can lead one to become a "bliss junky," who is always trying to find some substance or experience that will let them "go with the flow" and avoid persistently struggling in the face of adversity.

"Richness" is a heightened sense of awareness of the details of the present moment. This focus on the present, without distraction by thoughts of the future or memories of the past, allows for a lot more than the usual 120 bits of sensory information that we take in at once. Such a state is imbued with a sense of exceptional *significance*. However, Richness can cause one to dive too deeply, in a psychedelic sense, and get entranced by what one experiences at that depth or in that breadth of altered consciousness, so that one never comes up again and essentially drowns. This is similar to something called "the rapture of the deep" that is responsible for one in ten diving fatalities. At great depths, a diver has a euphoric sense of being one with the world that is produced by alterations in the gaseous chemistry of the lungs.

The psychobiology of this sense of oneness is now well understood, and it can be artificially replicated. It is now possible to measure, map, and produce the sense of "unity" or "absolute unitary being" or "oneness with the universe" so common to the mystical traditions of various religions. What is affected in these states is the right parietal lobe of the brain, which is responsible for our sense of location and navigation in space based on a judgment as to where our body ends, and the "external" world begins. This sense is impaired in people who suffer a stroke or brain damage. Studies have shown that it also becomes inhibited in those who experience such mystical states of oneness with everything. Intense concentration can short-circuit the right parietal lobe, blurring the boundary between self and other — or outright obliterating it, for a while.

Unfortunately, even some of the intellectual leaders of the Human Potential Movement are so lacking in discernment as to attribute both an ontological and an ethical significance to this sense of oneness. They make the mistake of thinking that it validates the metaphysics of personal consciousness [c] being ultimately identical to some putative Universal Consciousness [C]. This is the Atman equals Brahman construct that Gautama Buddha already deconstructed and revealed to be a sophisticated psychic projection, albeit one that does function as a powerful point of focus — including for the development of *siddhis,* or magical superpowers. Note, for example, this disastrously embarrassing passage in the book *Real Magic* by Dean Radin, Director of the Institute of Noetic Sciences, which, like Esalen, is based in California:

> 1. Consciousness is fundamental, meaning it is primary over the physical world. / 2. Everything is interconnected. / 3. There is only one Consciousness. / That's it. Those three ideas are the basis of real magic. / Those same ideas are also expounded in the various philosophies that assume there's ultimately just one "substance" underlying reality. Historically that substance has been called by many names: Spirit, Advaita, Brahman, Tao, Nirvana, Source, Yahweh, God, and numerous others.

Really? The Hindu "Brahman" is equal to the Buddhist "Nirvana," which is a "substance" equivalent to the Old Testament Hebrew conception of "Yahweh"? Wow. Just wow. The whole brunt of Gautama Buddha's ontology and epistemology is a deconstruction of the

Brahman projection, and of the kind of "substance" that Radin is equating with Nirvana here. As for Yahweh, he is a sadistically blood-thirsty, narcissistically jealous, and slave-driving warlord deity, who rides around in an aerial vehicle shaped like a column, terrorizing his believers into obedience, and commanding genocidal military campaigns such as the Siege of Jericho.

Radin is a parapsychologist, like Mishlove, and this Perennialist tendency is most egregious in the field of Parapsychology, which is spearheading an overthrow of the materialist paradigm that has been so dominant in the sciences for most of the modern age. A number of leading parapsychologists and associated thinkers in academic Philosophy are attempting to frame Monistic Idealism as the only legitimate alternative to materialism, should one want to avoid cynical Nihilism. They disingenuously disregard the fact that, as William James, the most philosophical of the founders of Parapsychology, himself believed, an ontology of Panpsychic Pluralism (like that of Prometheism) fits experimental findings of Extrasensory Perception (ESP) and Psychokinesis (PK) just as well, and it does so without sacrificing genuine human free will. Furthermore, the ethical framework of the so-called "Perennial Philosophy" or "Esoteric unity of all Tradition(s)," often also endorsed by Monistic Idealists in the Human Potential Movement, is not only a terribly ignorant take on the actual deep divergence of various world religions, but also an oppressively paternalistic and conservative worldview, even when hippies are "arguing" for it.

In the 1990s, the Human Potential Movement found a new nexus, at least a transient one, beyond the bastion of Esalen. This was the Burning Man festival in the Black Rock Desert of Nevada (three hours northeast of Reno). Burning Man actually began at a beach in San Francisco in the late 1980s, and then moved to the desert in 1990 after the event grew dramatically. Attending Burning Man is a rite of passage for Silicon Valley innovators, entrepreneurs, and executives. As Elon Musk said of Burning Man, "You could take the craziest L.A.

party and multiply it by a thousand, and it doesn't even get fucking close." Elon Musk came up with both his Solar City and Hyperloop designs while on "the playa," and he gave both away (in a gesture true to Burning Man culture).

The problem is that generals from the US Military also show up. Even the Supreme Commander of NATO has attended. The Pentagon has a huge camp that it sets up there called Camp PlayaGon, where high-ranking Pentagon officials mix with futurists and hackers. They run emergency Wi-Fi and livestream broadcasting services for the entire Burning Man event. Larry Page, the founder of Google, attends. Bear in mind that Google is, at this point, effectively an arm of the CIA. In 2013, Page said of Burning Man, "[It's] an environment where people can try new things. I think as technologists we should have some safe places where we can try out things and figure out the effect on society, the effect on people, without having to deploy it to the whole world." Also in attendance are senior vice presidents from Goldman Sachs, heads of the largest advertising agencies in the world, leaders of the World Economic Forum, all of whom come to Burning Man under fake names and with heavy security that sequesters them from the media and from mobs of regular attendees.

As a result, Burning Man is now probably the most heavily surveilled event penetrated by US intelligence and security services. A dozen different state and federal agencies bring millions of dollars of high-tech spy gear to the event, from infrared goggles to tactical vehicles. Armies of undercover agents are canvassing the entire playa. Recently released, and heavily redacted, FBI documents acquired through the Freedom of Information Act reveal that the Bureau has conducted an intelligence and infiltration program at Burning Man for years now. The program is based on the old FBI COINTELPRO tactics from the '60s and '70s that were used to penetrate, compromise, and misdirect groups such as the Black Panthers, Students for a Democratic Society, and the American Indian Movement. They extensively use agent provocateurs to destabilize groups at Burning Man from within, or to set them up. In the past five years, arrests by plainclothes and undercover agents at the Burning Man festival were up by over 1,000 percent from its early years. The event is, after all, held on a stretch of desert that is under the jurisdiction of the U.S. Bureau of Land Management. To believe that Burning Man is some kind of "Temporary Autonomous Zone," in the sense that Peter Lamborn Wilson meant that term, is perversely delusional.

In their book *Stealing Fire*, Kotler and Wheal repeatedly use the phrase "Promethean" and even "Promethean revolution" to describe the open-source access to a proliferation of methods to induce STER. It is supposedly Promethean because the Human Potential Movement has largely removed middlemen and established religious institutions from standing between oneself and whatever techniques can lead to an expansion or deepening of consciousness. This is the proverbial "stealing of fire" from various overlords that their book title refers to. The more people can access altered states, the less likely it is that any potential cult leader can build a movement around his personal "revelations" from having experienced such states.

The proliferation and personalization of epiphanies could be considered Promethean. However, the problem with their position is revealed when they slip up in lines like this one, where they are discussing "hedonic calendaring" or the necessity of figuring out how often one should let oneself "get into the zone." Kotler and Wheal write: "By balancing inebriated abandon with monklike sobriety, ribald sexuality with introspective celibacy, and extreme risk-taking with cozy domesticity, you'll create more contrast and spot patterns sooner. … Attach the hiatus to traditional seasons of forbearance—Lent, Yom Kippur, Ramadan—or impose your own." Lent, Yom Kippur, or Ramadan? Really? That is more or less equivalent to, and interchangeable with, "impose your own"! Judeo-Christianity and Islam are options equal to a Promethean individualist spirituality?

The core of the problem goes back to the basic ideology, or lack thereof, upon which Esalen was founded. The point of departure of the Esalen worldview is that tools—or techniques—that alter consciousness are more important than beliefs. These would include "meditation, biofeedback, yoga, ritual, isolation tanks, tantric sex, breathwork, martial arts, group dynamics and drugs..." That all sounds great, on the face of it. But dig a bit deeper. Some years before becoming the Chairman of the Board at Esalen, Jeffrey Kripal had written a tome about Esalen and its place in the history of American spirituality. The title of the book says everything. In *Esalen: America's Religion of No Religion*, Kripal writes of the Human Potential Movement that "[i]t has no official alliance with any religious system. It can provide, like a kind of American Mystical Constitution, a spiritual space where almost any religious form can flourish, provided… that it does not… claim to speak for everyone. As an early Esalen motto put it, 'No one captures the flag.'"

That's nice, until Chinese Confucianists, Islamic fundamentalists, or, in America, most likely Christian Evangelicals literally "capture the flag" of a country whose Counter Culture has no cohesive and well-defined ethos of its own, on the basis of which such regressive forces can be resisted. There are also regressive forces from within, such as Black Lives Matter (BLM) and other identity politics groups that are being enlisted in a controlled demolition of our civilization. It is no wonder that, a couple of years after refusing to write me that updated letter, Kripal wholeheartedly embraced Critical Race Theory to the point of restructuring his entire university course on the paranormal and the sacred around it. In his latest book, *The Superhumanities* (2022), Kripal begins by expressing his guilt over being white and professing a newfound interest in "Afrofuturism." He had the poster for his class at Rice redone to feature Black Panther and to advertise it as a class as much on "race" and "sex" (meaning gender politics) as on religious studies.

In December of 2020, Black Lives Matter destroyed my Alma Mater, the Dalton School, by totally deconstructing and reconstructing its curriculum and culture around Critical Race Theory. In *The*

Superhumanities, which was written in 2020 at the height of BLM, Kripal expresses his unequivocal support for such identity politics agendas being implemented at educational institutions. What kind of reforms are Critical Race Theorists implementing? Well, "ethno-mathematics training" for example, according to which it is racist to correct black kids if they think that 2+2 equals 5. Another example is denying white students an education in Shakespeare or the Classics because a black student might be "triggered." I am always taken aback by how Conservatives or people on the Right refer to these CRT Identitarians as "Communists." Can you imagine Stalin, who beat America in the space race while he was in power, compromising the math education of Russian kids to appease embarrassed, underperforming non-white minorities in the USSR? Blacks remain only 13% of the US population. Another CRT policy is to deny advanced placement (AP) education to all students at high schools, such as Dalton, simply because not as many non-white students qualify for it, per their population, as whites do. Meanwhile, they are punishing all of the white kids (most of whom, at Dalton, are Ashkenazi Jews) with high aptitude by getting rid of the entire AP program.

People like Kripal do not realize that identity politics, both racial and religious, is more likely to be used to ultimately undermine "progressive" aims than to help in achieving them. There has been a tendency for former hippies, such as the American poet Charles Upton, to come from out of the vacuum of values in this Counter Culture and turn into Traditionalists, embracing as their reactionary "identity" one or another regressively conservative "vessel" of the *Sophia Perennis* (Eternal Wisdom) such as Islam (albeit in the guise of Sufism). Of course, Traditionalists would deny that they are Identitarians, but with their apartheid-style "stay in your own ghetto" view of religious and culture identity, they are actually Mega-Identitarians. BLM is child's play. One can see the convergence of the two types of discourse in a 'thinker' like Alexander Dugin, who advocates Traditionalism while also embracing all anti-Western identity politics movements.

I mentioned Upton, in particular, because after he was awarded with the Bigelow Grand Prize by Kripal, and he unlisted every one of the 37 video interviews that we had recorded together over the span of five years, Jeffrey Mishlove invited Charles Upton to come onto *New Thinking Allowed* in an ongoing series of interviews platforming and promoting Traditionalism. He urged viewers to buy and read all of Upton's books, while platforming Upton to directly attack Prometheus as a quintessentially Satanic figure, emulation of whom will lead people to damnation. In every single one of these NTA interviews, Upton sat there on camera in front of a placard behind his head that reads *La ilaha illa Allah*, "there is no God but Allah," the Muslim testimony of faith.

Upton certainly subscribes to the Muslim conception of God, which is the most oppressively totalitarian in the entire religious history of mankind. God, or Allah, is both omnipotent and omniscient. Not only does God have foreknowledge of everything that must happen, including anything anyone is ever going to do, nothing happens that is not an expression of the will of God, and that is not of a piece with the Being of God.

Upton sees time travel and reincarnation as connected, and he rejects both of them on the basis of his belief that each one of us is inseparable from the place and time in which we are ensconced as an illusory temporal expression of a facet of God's eternal Being. To his mind, allowing time travel as a possibility would be heresy because it would mean that any potential time traveler has enough autonomy as an individual to extricate himself from a particular epoch and possibly even revise history, meaning that the time traveler has a will of his own apart from God and could work against the will of God as expressed in the inevitable events of history. Likewise, reincarnation cannot be admitted because it also gives the soul too much autonomy in distinction from God and epochal history conceived as an expression of God's eternal will in illusory time. Upton outright claims that both the belief in time travel and the belief in reincarnation are diabolical attempts to evade being answerable to God's judgment after death, by trying to give oneself any number of second chances or do-overs.

Although here he faces the typical problem of evil, namely how it is that any of us can be responsible for anything at all if God is almighty. His answer is simply that free will is a mystery, and that we can never know how what we feel ourselves to be willing is actually exactly what God had willed. This is, of course, a piece of sheer nonsense, and is particularly hypocritical in light of Upton's claim that we ought not to be fascinated by mysteries or entertain anything mysterious that prevents us from reaching closure with regard to knowledge of a subject—a line of argument he uses to argue against certain trends in Ufology, without accepting the same standards with regard to his Theology.

Evil is, according to Upton, a lack of reality or a "hole in Being." First of all, if that is the case, God cannot be an omnipotent, omniscient, and perfect Being of the kind that Upton claims. Secondly, if evil is only unreality and a void with no positive identity, then what is the ontological status of Satan, the Jinn (i.e., demons), and the Antichrist that Upton is so obsessed with in his writings on the Counter-Initiation and UFO Disclosure? Are they real, meaning ontologically substantial, or aren't they? If they aren't, then the reams that he has written on not falling prey to their deceptions is rendered nonsensical. Unlike Zoroastrians, Upton does not leave himself the possibility that such "evil" beings are ontologically substantial and separate from a good God who is mighty and wise enough to *eventually* triumph over them. No, he cannot accept any limitation on God. Ahura Mazda allows for too much free will and is not a totalitarian enough God for him.

Obviously, it is not lost on me that, as a Traditionalist and proponent of the so-called Perennial "Philosophy" Upton is drawing from the Neo-Platonic conception of the gradation of the great chain of Being. But this classical philosophical attempt to reconcile the finite and infinite, the relative and the absolute, is incoherent in itself, and attempting to synthesize it with both Abrahamic and Vedic theology renders it even more muddled. According to Upton, who is basing himself here, as elsewhere, on René Guénon and other Traditionalists, there are eight levels of existence, in descending fashion: Godhead, Being, Intellect, Archangelic, Angelic, Imaginal, Etheric, and Material. These can be further categorized in terms of four over-arching qualities of phenomena, with the first two being Divine, the second two Spiritual, the next two being Psychic (so that angels are entities operating on the psychic plane of the Imaginal Realm), and the last two being material—wherein the etheric is supposedly the occulted energetic essence of material nature, rather than something truly psychic, let alone spiritual. Aside from how arbitrary this categorization is, there are two huge problems with it. Firstly, from a logical standpoint, let me reiterate that it is not compatible with a fully self-consistent Monism regarding the putatively perfect Being of God. Parmenides already spoke the last word on this at the dawn of Philosophy. If one admits The One as Reality, the rest of the perceived finitude of being, however we feel ourselves inclined to categorize it, is sheer delusion and a tale told by an idiot. Secondly, there is not a shred of empirical evidence to support this whole scheme.

We certainly have evidence, from Parapsychology, that there is a psychic or etheric dimension to phenomena. But that what may be called "psychic" is any different from the "etheric" or that either of these is truly distinct from the "material" (rather than just being another state or modality of it) is not something that can be empirically demonstrated, let alone the existence of so-called "spiritual" and "divine" realms beyond the "merely psychic." Radically empiricist rejection of such abstractions is not a Modern heresy either, indicative of the Satanic agenda of Modernity, as Upton would have us believe. Nor is it unique to Prometheism. Rather, it is a major thrust in the ontological and epistemological teachings of Gautama Buddha, some twenty-five centuries ago. Just as he admitted the efficacy of psychic powers and related his own experiences of etheric phenomena, Buddha rejected the substantial reality of any higher spiritual realms and of anything like the existence of God (Brahman).

As a Traditionalist or Perennialist, Upton needs to adamantly deny this fact. According to Traditionalism or the Sophia Perennis, all "world religions" such as Judeo-Christianity, Islam, Hinduism, and Buddhism express the same Primordial Tradition. They are not only compatible with one another; they are each an expression of the Divine Will as made manifest through the sages and prophets of these traditions. Just so that there is no confusion here, Upton is most certainly not claiming that there can be One World Religion. Any attempt to devise some syncretic "Primordialism" or "Perennialism" as a single coherent faith is in his view "Satanic," and every attempt at this, from those that took place in the cosmopolitan Hellenistic world, to those of the contemporary New Age, are diabolical machinations to lead people astray.

What is worse yet is an attempt to present such a syncretic One World Religion in scientific garb, using the latest discoveries in Quantum Physics or Parapsychology to unify science and religion. According to Upton, this attempt to warp "objective science" by having scientific research enter the domain of psychism or etheric phenomena is absolutely Satanic. In other words, Upton affirms that artificial distinction between the Spiritual and a purely materialist and reductionist Science, which in *Prometheus and Atlas* I took great pains to show was deliberately set up by the Jesuit Order so as to protect Church dogma from the nascent European Enlightenment. Upton affirms this Jesuit conception of the limits of proper "objective science," just as he follows René Guénon in claiming that when this materialist science that was characteristic of the early Modern age is abandoned in favor of a "cosmic psychism" and a penetration of science into the occult, then we have passed from mere "Anti-Tradition" into the "Counter-Tradition" of fully flowered Modernity (with the exception that Upton refers to the latter as Postmodernity, as I also did in *Prometheus and Atlas*, albeit affirmatively, calling for a Positive Postmodernity).

The appearance of the Scientific World Religion, in other words my Prometheism, marks the arrival of the Antichrist or *Al-Dajjal* as Muslims call him. Prometheism, in particular, has all of the characteristics that merit being branded as this "quasi-scientific" gospel of the Antichrist, because it is explicitly and emphatically evolutionary. Upton rejects the theory of evolution. Not just Darwin's theory of evolution, but *any* theory of evolution. He thinks that human nature is a fixed idea in the mind of God, one which of course includes a definite gender distinction (with roles appropriate to men and women), and he believes that apes are devolved men rather than that men ever evolved from anything like apes.

According to Upton, who is just being a good Traditionalist here, the very idea of Progress that is at the heart of any type of Futurism is a deluded collapse of Being's hierarchy in a horizontal direction. He thinks that the hierarchical levels of existence up to the perfection of God have been made to collapse into a sequential progression to a putative utopian perfection projected into the future. Actually, this is not just a delusion. He claims it is the word of demons. To believe that things are better than they ever were in the past, in large part because of science, or to harbor the conceit that we can strive to make the world even better in the future, through continued technological advancement and greater scientific knowledge, is to be subject to demonic deception aimed at damning our souls to hellish divine retribution.

In fact, most Traditionalists believe that history is an epochal succession of declining world ages, with each more degenerate than the last, until the Divine Order is spectacularly restored at the end of the world, although this is another point of major incoherence within Traditionalism in its attempt to reconcile Apocalyptically-oriented Abrahamic religions with Eastern religions that have a cyclical view of time and world ages. Folks like Upton try to syncretize the Kalki

Avatar with the Second Coming of Christ and the arrival of the Imam Mahdi. Where would Maitreya Buddha fit in? Would he also stand beside Imam Mahdi, just as Imam Mahdi is supposed to be shoulder to shoulder with Jesus Christ, who somehow *is* the Kalki Avatar? Absurdities upon absurdities.

Traditionalists believe that one must adhere to one or another world religion in its orthodox form, without deviation, if one wishes to have a living relationship with the Sophia Perennis. It is an apartheid theology. Separate but equal, or maybe not so equal at all in the end, since, like Guénon, Upton determined Islam to be the most pristine and perfect of the remaining vessels of the Primordial Tradition. This leaves him with the problem of trying to reconcile certain aspects of Vedic and Buddha Dharma—or even Christian Mysticism—with the kind of totalitarian theology that Islam espouses and that is paradigmatic for Traditionalism. This can, to a certain extent, be done with Judeo-Christianity and Hinduism, although as noted above, with Hinduism there is the problem of reincarnation, which Traditionalists like Upton need to reinterpret as an affinity between different souls living in disparate epochs. When one has what appear to be "past life memories," that is supposedly just psychic resonance with a similar past individual. Never mind that extensive empirical investigation of reincarnation by scientists such as Dr. Ian Stevenson totally puts the lie to this claim. But Buddhism is a much bigger problem, *especially* in its orthodox form (and Traditionalists prefer the orthodox forms of religions).

Atheism is part of the fundamental teaching of Gautama Buddha regarding *anatta* or the lack of any inherent essence or substantial being, whether of God or the Self. For this reason and others, at the inception of the Traditionalist school in the early twentieth century, there was an argument over whether Buddhism should be considered a legitimate "world religion" that expresses the Primordial Tradition alongside Judeo-Christianity, Islam, and Hinduism. Ananda Coomaraswamy infamously reversed himself on this, first rejecting and then accepting Buddha into the fold of sages and prophets. Of course, Upton never mentions this embarrassing episode in the history of Traditionalism. He is content to adopt the preposterously ignorant theological position of the Traditionalist school in total disregard of the vast differences and deep divergences in the theologies of various sects of major religions, let alone between those religions taken as a whole.

Nor does he want to entertain, even for a moment, the idea that "world religions" often became that through brute force, such as certainly is the case with the Muslim faith that he prefers above all others. Given other concrete historical circumstances, totally different cults may have been able to fight their way into the club of accepted "world religions." No, for Upton, it was always God's will that only Judeo-Christianity, Islam, Hinduism, and Buddhism be the great facets of the Sophia Perennis. It could never have been Zoroastrianism, or Mithraism, or Odinism, or Taoism. Let alone UFO cults like the Raelians — and heaven forbid that we should ever take seriously the argument (based on extensive evidence) that Judeo-Christianity, Islam, and Hinduism themselves were engineered through manipulative Close Encounters, and that the UFO attempts to engineer religions did not stop there but continued, for example, with Mormonism, albeit with less success due to the Counter-Traditional ethos of Modernity. Joseph Smith's encounters with the "angel" Moroni (Moron I?) fit the phenomenology of Close Encounters as clearly as the so-called "Miracle of the Sun" and the "visions" of the three shepherd children at Fatima in 1917.

Upton rants about the lurid and grotesque quality of Close Encounter reports, especially abductions, calling them excrement that is pulled out of a magician's hat. He thinks that it is blasphemy to compare these types of experiences to religious encounters and "miracles," as even a Ufologist of the caliber of Jacques Vallée does. Upton adopts the Platonist definition of God as not just Truth and Justice, but also Beauty. The Divine is supreme Beauty and expresses itself in the

Beautiful, so the ugliness of UFO encounters cannot be divine. Wait, but wasn't God supposed to be an omnipotent and omniscient all-encompassing perfect Being? Oops. No, the Close Encounters studied by Ufologists are diabolical deceptions produced by demons, or evil *Jinn* to use the Muslim term. Upton explicitly states that these are the "fallen angels" of the Bible, but in accordance with Muslim belief and in line with the Traditionalist theology set forth by René Guénon and his successors, they are not material beings. Rather, they are beings from the etheric plane—not even the psychic plane or imaginal realm. One ought not to confuse them with angels, simply because angels and anything spiritual or psychic must also enter the material world by crossing through the etheric plane.

New Age science and spirituality, the fusion of which was epitomized, in Upton's view, by Jack Parsons, is a movement wherein the self-will of individuals to storm Heaven by their own initiative, through individualized esoteric or occult practice, or through a scientific approach to the psychic, is putting cracks in "the great wall" of the etheric plane. Supposedly the materialism of the early Modern age first solidified this wall between the material plane and higher spiritual realms, so that later on the hardened and more brittle wall could be cracked *but from beneath,* thereby letting infra-psychic or etheric forces of a malevolent nature into the material plane in the form of UFO aliens who carry out horrific abductions that are just demonic assaults in a new quasi-scientific form. According to Upton, the whole thing is a diabolical plot that will only end with the sudden opening of the great wall or barrier from above, at the Second Coming of Christ as Kalki the Avatar, together with the Imam Mahdi.

As I demonstrated in *Closer Encounters* (2021), my monumental study of the UFO phenomenon, this distinction that Upton draws between the lurid and grotesquely ugly quality of encounters with "aliens," on the one hand, and biblical or Vedic accounts of human interactions with angels or Daevas, on the other hand, is totally arbitrary and unsupported by the details of scriptural accounts as compared to empirical evidence from Ufology. We are dealing with *exactly* the same phenomenon involving *precisely* the same beings. Moreover, all of the manipulative deception and traumatic abuse that Upton identifies as part of the UFO abduction literature is what the Abrahamic angels or Vedic gods have used in order to create these so-called "world religions" that are enslaving systems of mass mind control. Both the "subliminal contradiction" and the "deferred closure" that Upton fingers as psychological warfare tactics involved in the UFO "Disclosure Deception" are methodologies of producing cognitive dissonance and irrational faith in a Stockholm Syndrome-type abuser that I have discerned at work in the entire history of religious so-called "revelation." For Upton to accuse Ufologists, government officials, and "black magicians" like Parsons of this, without seeing that the worst examples of it are in the careers of Moses, Jesus, and Muhammad, is sheer hypocrisy. Go read my exegesis of the actual content of Genesis, Exodus, and the books of various prophets, such as Ezekiel, in Chapter 6 of *Closer Encounters*. Or, for that matter, the passages of Hindu texts, such as the *Mahabharata,* that read as if they could be parts of a narrative from Ufology.

Upton's aesthetic judgment against the putatively demonic beings responsible for "alien abduction" and other encounters with UFOs can be directed against scripture with at least equal force, and in fact, when one does so, one realizes that those who are standing for Justice and against tyranny in the Bible are the Fallen Angels. Or, to put it in Hindu terms, the "demonic" Asuras who revolt against the Devas. The beings that Upton, as a self-professed and devout Muslim, generally prefers to call "the Jinn" who are in revolt against Allah. The Jinn who, Upton admits, once had their own society on the face of the Earth. Namely, Atlantis, the antediluvian civilization that was punished for its Promethean pride.

CHAPTER 4

BELIAL OF ATLANTIS

If we want to dynamite Traditionalism at its foundation, as I do, then we need to ask the question of where, or when, the Counter-Tradition really began. Even if René Guénon saw the Counter-Initiation as coming to its culmination in Modernity, he also recognized that Modernity is not so much a particular epoch as it is a form of society. Was there, as Guénon himself suggests at times, a Modernity before the modern age? An ancient or primordial modernity? Indeed, there was, and it is there, or then, that we will find the origin of the Counter-Tradition. This primordial modernity of "Atlantis" has been hidden from us by "the gods" precisely because what defined the character of that society was, above all, a Promethean rebellion that is the most original and authentic form of Counter-Traditionalism.

In approaching this subject, we face the problem that has been endemic to studies of groups such as the Gnostics or the Assassins. We are forced, for the most part, to reconstruct their worldview and way of life based upon the hostile heresiology of the Catholic Church or the Caliphate. Of all the sources concerning the rebels in Atlantis, on account of whose rebellion the civilization was supposedly destroyed, only Plato is somewhat neutral. The rest of our sources are vehemently hostile and literally demonize the rebel Atlanteans, seeing them as the first host of Satan. This is consistent with the biblical Books of Genesis and Enoch, through to the accounts of Rudolf Steiner, who calls the rebels "Ahrimanic," and the Sunday school teacher Edgar Cayce, who brands them "the sons of Belial," rising in opposition to the putatively divine so-called "Law of One."

Of course, there is one other source here that is supremely relevant and that is the myth of Prometheus—including the parts of it involving his brothers Atlas and Epimetheus (as well as the latter's wife, Pandora) and the son of Prometheus, Deucalion, who is the Greek Noah. In order to really understand Cayce's "Belial" group, which Steiner brands as "Ahrimanic," on its own terms through a reconstruction of its own perspective, we need to identify convergences in the various "Atlantis" or "Fallen Angel" narratives, establish the terminological equivalents across these narratives, and extract the core elements of this occulted history from the moralistic propaganda that has hitherto enmeshed them. Then the story can be reread through the lens of the mythos and ethos of the Promethean rebellion.

There are a handful of key elements to this story, which are common to every significant version of it, and which very likely point to a hidden history that haunts our world to this day. The first element is that long, long ago, the world of mortals was much more directly administered by "gods" or "angels." These seemingly "immortal" beings hid "heavenly secrets" from mere mortals, who served these divine beings more or less as a race of slaves, ignorant of the purposes and motivations of their masters. Plato calls these masters the Olympian gods. In Genesis and in the Book of Enoch, which was later removed from the Bible because it revealed too much, they are referred to as the Elohim. Not incidentally, there is a direct Hindu equivalent of this plural Hebrew word, which literally means "the Shining ones," namely the Devas or Devis, the gods and goddesses who can be seen as the Indian equivalent of the Olympians, since the Greeks and the Indians were originally part of the same Indo-European community. (How the revolutionary worldview of the Iranian branch of this community fits into the religious conflict at the core of Atlantean society is a significant question that we will come to momentarily, in a critique of Steiner's use of the term "Ahrimanic" to refer to the rebel Atlanteans.)

In any case, the second element of the story that remains consistent across all of our sources is that, at a certain point, there was hybridization between the immortals and the mortals. The Greek sources, including Plato, refer to the hybrids as "heroes"—a word that originally derives from *eros*, namely erotic love, between gods and humans. In Plato's account of Atlantis, the hybrids are heirs of Poseidon who have human mothers, including Poseidon's eldest son, King Atlas, after whom "Atlantis" is named "the realm of Atlas." According to Plato, as these hybrids themselves mated with other mortals, and the human element in them was amplified, while they still retained a godlike aspect, they were filled with prideful ambition and irreverence toward the gods. The Hebrew sources, both Genesis 6 and the much lengthier account in the Book of Enoch, which seems to have been excised from this cryptic and clearly abridged part of the Bible, refer to these hybrids as "Nephilim" or giants, the "great men of renown." They are the offspring of about two hundred Elohim (angels) known as "the Watchers" or Observers, presumably Overseers of mankind, who broke ranks with the divine hierarchy and came down to Earth to take mortal women as their wives. Later Christian sources will refer to the fathers of these hybrids as "the fallen angels" since, as the Book of Enoch explains, they were punished for this transgression by being banished from Heaven and bound underneath the Earth until the Apocalypse, when they will wage a final battle with God.

The third element that cuts across every "Atlantis" or "Fallen Angel" narrative is that the "divine beings" who mated with mortal women revealed all kinds of knowledge to these women, and the men who were their offspring, which the chief of the gods (Zeus, or the Biblical "Adonai Elohim") had secreted away from mankind. When we read the Eden narrative in the Book of Genesis with attention to the phraseology of the original Hebrew, and without Judeo-Christian biases, it is clear that the chief of the gods does so out of jealousy and fear that mortals would become the equals of the gods if they were to have access to this forbidden knowledge. Moreover, the figure of the serpent, who is punished by having his legs removed for revealing this knowledge to Eve, is clearly the same being referred to in the Apocalypse of St. John as "the Dragon," namely Satan, the "adversary" of God. In fact, the Book of Revelations clearly identifies the Dragon as "that serpent of old."

If we read these passages from the beginning and end of the Bible through the lens of the Fallen Angel narrative that leads up to the destruction of the antediluvian civilization of "sinners" against the divine order, we can clearly see that the rebel angels in the Book of Enoch are a more elaborate version of the knowledge-bringers symbolized in the Eden story by the Satanic serpent or Dragon — the Dragon who, like the insurgent Watchers, will break free from a subterranean prison for a final battle with God at the end of days. Eve, in Eden, is symbolic of the fact that it was women who, in the first place, received the forbidden knowledge from Heaven. As the Book of Enoch explains, these women, the mothers of the hybrids, became powerful sorceresses, priestesses, and mothers of increasingly irreverent and ambitious demigods on Earth. These are the men who Plato holds responsible for the rebellion of Atlantis against the world order of Olympus.

This theme of the unauthorized revelation to mankind of secret knowledge of occulted arts and crafts, namely of science and technology belonging to the gods, is at the core of the myth of Prometheus and allows us to discern how that tragic tale is inextricable from the tragedy of Atlantis. As I have already explained, it is not a mere coincidence that the eldest son of Poseidon, namely Atlas, the first King of Atlantis, after whom the realm is named, has the same name as the brother of Prometheus, the titan Atlas. Poseidon, who not incidentally (as we see in Homer) from the depths of the ocean is working at cross-purposes to Zeus, and whose chief implement, the trident, becomes the staff of Satan. As I argued in *Prometheus and Atlas* (Arktos 2016), the reason why the son of Poseidon and Cleito has the same name as the titan Atlas is because, as Plato himself suggests by coupling the account of Atlantis in *Critias* with that of the demiurge in *Timaeus*, the archetypally defining qualities of the titan Atlas are also characteristic of the sovereign principle of Atlantis—or at least of the rebel Atlanteans.

Like his brother Prometheus, Atlas defies Zeus. The image of him bearing the world on his shoulders is less an image of punishment, as the Olympian theologians would have us believe, and more an image of bearing responsibility for governing the whole world. It is closely connected to why "Atlas" became the term for maps of the world, not just of the Earth but star maps of the heavens. Like the fire of the secret science and technology stolen from Olympus by Prometheus and gifted to mankind, this is a symbol of godlike knowledge and a perspective over the world as if from outside of it. According to Plato, Atlantis conquered the world through its titanic ocean-going navy, and mariners navigated using the stars.

Then there is the fact that Deucalion, the son of Prometheus, is essentially the Greek version of Noah, who attempts to save a portion of mankind from the flood that Zeus unleashes in order to destroy rebellious Atlantis and its global maritime empire. As I explained in Chapter 2, in the Greek version of the story, instead of saving people on the orders of the same chief god who brings the flood, which makes no sense whatsoever, Deucalion is aligned with his father Prometheus, whose enlightenment of mankind is what ultimately triggers such a tyrannical response from the gods. The biblical version of the story is trying to cover this up, with the end result that Yahweh, the chief of the Elohim, just seems like a schizophrenic or bipolar lunatic who capriciously decides to both destroy and save mankind.

Finally, there is the part of the myth of Prometheus that involves his other brother, Epimetheus, and the gift of Pandora—the Greek "Eve." This also attests to the fact that the Prometheus tragedy and the story of Atlantis are two versions of the same "myth" that preserves a memory of occulted human prehistory. According to the myth of

Prometheus, it is Prometheus, not Zeus, who fashioned humanity. He did it with the help of his brother, Epimetheus. However, Epimetheus, the forgetful one whose name means "afterthought," neglected to assign an essence to man as he had done when he created all of the other animals. It bears repeating that this is a profound symbol of the fact that human existence precedes any essence, and that man is left to define himself, lacking anything like what some would want to believe is a fixed and predetermined "human nature." Prometheus stealing the fire of the forge of technological science from Olympus is actually a remedy for this lack of essence, insofar as *techne* is a means whereby man can not only remake his world but remake himself as he sees fit. The way in which Zeus is threatened by the creation of Prometheus, fearing that this new race of men might supplant the Olympian gods rather than serve them, parallels the Sumerian story of Enki's creation of humanity and his championing the cause of men against the god Enlil, who wants to reduce mankind to a race of slaves subjugated by the Anunnaki.

In any case, the point is that Zeus retaliates against the theft of heavenly fire by Prometheus when he gives the "gift" of Pandora to the titan's foolish brother, Epimetheus, who accepts the "first woman" despite Prometheus having warned his brother not to accept any "gifts" from Zeus. As has already been noted, by implication, this aspect of the Prometheus myth suggests that the race of mortals fashioned by Prometheus was not yet sexually differentiated. In that earlier discussion I suggested that we would be mistaken to conclude that it was a race consisting only of men, and that Pandora was literally the first woman, because if we look back at Plato and other early Greek authors, we see that the Greeks believed that primordial mortals were androgynous or hermaphroditic. This aligns completely with a fourth element of the Atlantis narrative that is especially clear in the accounts of Rudolf Steiner and, even more so, Edgar Cayce. Namely that sexual differentiation came into being during the course of Atlantean history, and that the Atlanteans started out being sexually undifferentiated.

So, there is a whole other dimension to the illicit revelation of forbidden knowledge by the dissident "divine beings" to *women*, in particular, women with whom they have sex to engender a godless race of supermen. The language of mythology is often confused and convoluted, being a preservation of forgotten or occulted history in the sub-rational collective unconscious of one or another society. People who read mythology as if it is a literary narrative, akin to the works of Tolkien, simply because the latter also has archetypal power, are utterly ignorant of the gulf that separates true mythology, with its mimetic transmission, from consciously constructed literature. The myth of Pandora, and the box or jar of woes she brings with her, as a punishment for the transgression of Prometheus, is the same myth as the original sin of Eve, which is in turn the same myth as the seduction of women by the Fallen Angels. It is the myth whose prehistoric substrate both Rudolf Steiner and Edgar Cayce are fathoming anew in their mediumistic accounts of the connection between sexual differentiation, transgressive sex, and forbidden knowledge in the rise and fall of Atlantis.

The nexus of these associations is a conception of the connection between Eros and Sophia that is a Western alchemical equivalent to the Indian idea of Tantra, which orthodox Hindus have branded as the "Ashuric" path or the *adharma* ("lawlessness") associated with the Ashuras—those titans at war with the gods. According to Hindu mythology, "evil" comes into the world with the Ashuras but a close examination of Hindu scriptures and epics reveals no specific differentiation between the gods and titans that would justify the designation of one class of these superhuman beings as moral and the other as immoral. The Ashuras are "evil" and are responsible for the "evils" that follow from their rebellion against the gods simply because they are disrupting the divine order and thereby unleashing violent chaos. A divine order which, I might add, takes the form of an extremely rigid hierarchical caste system.

Steiner identifies the highest religious and political authority of the pre-rebellion Atlantean society as Manu, a name adopted by a line of priest-kings, which is preserved by Hindus in their *Laws of Manu*—a compendium of orthodox law and order that sanctifies the caste system. In anticipation of, or alignment with, Traditionalist theological discourse, Steiner refers to the Second Coming of Christ as the Manu of the Future, who is supposed to be willingly and consciously embraced by mankind rather than being unconsciously followed like the Manus in the early days of Atlantis. Traditionalists say the same of the Muslim Imam Mahdi.

This reaches back to the first of the aforementioned elements of the Atlantis myth that is common to every narrative about the antediluvian civilization, namely that its "uncorrupted" structure was a pyramidal hierarchy with its capstone as the gods in the Heavens and its base as subhuman laborers on Earth. Both Rudolf Steiner and Edgar Cayce, each using their own terminology, affirm this hierarchy (*heiros arche*, "holy order") and morally justify it with a metaphysics and cosmology that is, for all intents and purposes, indistinguishable from the theology of Traditionalism (regardless of whether the Traditionalists are comfortable with having Steiner and Cayce in their ranks). According to Steiner and Cayce, the early Atlanteans, like mortals on Earth in general, were lacking in individuality, conscientious reflection, and willful self-determination. They had a collective consciousness or group mind, and they were not just guided, but led, very directly, by gurus and god-kings, who were "divine messengers" or representatives of the gods themselves. Mankind itself was internally differentiated into various classes or castes of people, with more or less access to divine guidance. Those few mortals with the most access belonged to Mystery Schools, wherein they would be initiated into some of the lesser or lower secrets belonging to the gods and thereby become privy to only those parts of the divine plan for which they had a "need to know" so as to help the gods unfold it. This "father knows best" system could also be characterized as "ancestor worship," since it was based entirely on a powerful memory of how things have always been done by the pious and sagacious forefathers, and must continue to be done, with no capacity for conscious reflection, rational analysis, or creative innovation.

However, at a certain point, perhaps on account of the aforementioned hybridization or attendant to it, the lightbulb went on in a certain portion of the Atlantean population. They started to think for themselves and develop a sense of personal identity. According to Cayce and Steiner, an attempt was made by the Messengers of the Mysteries to accommodate this evolutionary leap by guiding these people into a more rational acceptance of the same divine standards of morality and proper conduct that had hitherto been accepted unconsciously or, as it were, in a kind of mesmeric state. While this may have worked for some people, marking the beginning of the first schools of rational theology based on justification of the order ordained by the gods from on high, there was an increasingly large subset of Atlanteans who essentially called "bullshit" on this entire scheme. These are the rebels that Edgar Cayce refers to as "the sons of Belial" and that Rudolf Steiner characterizes as "Ahrimanic." Let us go into an analysis and deconstruction of each of these characterizations for the same group of rebel Atlanteans, the partisans of Prometheus.

The word *Belial* is a Hebrew contraction of two words. The first is *beli-*, meaning "without." The second is disputed amongst scholars, some of whom contend that it is *-ya'al*, meaning "to be of value," others argue that the second half of the compound word is *-ol*, meaning "yoke, or binding," and lastly some who say that it is *-el* or "god." This ambiguity is actually perfectly appropriate because it yields three potential meanings of the word *Belial*, all of which are legitimate characterizations of the group that Edgar Cayce dutifully demonizes, Sunday school teacher and Christian preacher that he is. We could think of these several meanings as the three prongs of Satan's scepter—originally the trident of Poseidon, the forefather of Atlantis.

Beli–ya'al would mean "without value." Later usages in the Bible misunderstand this to be a reference to "worthless" men, later further degraded to "naughty" men, whereas what was originally and more literally being said was that these men were without a standard of value. They did not believe in the objectivity of morality. *Beli–ol* would mean "yokeless" or "unbound." In this connection, two very important theological terms are relevant. Firstly, the word *religion* itself comes from *religere,* which means "to bind." Secondly, the word *yoga* also means "to yoke." Thus, the *Beli-ol* are irreligious people who are not yoked to the putatively "divine" order, what in Sanskrit is called *Rta* (divinely ordained cosmic order). The Tantric term *adharma* would also convey this "yokeless" or "unbound" character. Finally, *Beli-el* would mean "without god," in other words, without *any* belief in a god or reverence for gods situated in some station above or beyond us. Atheists are usually materialists, but the Belial group were spectral atheists. (This is also true of Buddhists. In proper Buddhist teaching, "gods" can refer to either archetypes, egregores, or superhuman but finite and ultimately mortal beings, and none of these three things are "gods" in a genuinely theistic sense.) So, in sum, *Belial* means godless, lawless, and unbound. It is not the name of an entity, as it was later misunderstood to be. Belial is only "Satan" in the sense that *Satan,* another Hebrew word, is an adjective meaning "adversary" or "opposition" to the divine order. Belial is not some demonic entity, but the Belial group is Satanic. (I do not call them "the sons of Belial" because this is a translation of a Hebrew stock phrase that just means "heirs of" and it is clear from Cayce's own account that women, including "priestesses" or sorceresses, in the Belial group were at least as prominent as men.)

Steiner refers to the Belial group as "Ahrimanic." Being a scholar of Iranian Studies, I cannot but remark on how this is one of the most demented and warped misidentifications that I have ever come across in theological literature. Steiner himself fully acknowledges the ancient Iranian matrix for his use of the term "Ahrimanic" to describe the dissidents in Atlantis. However, he misunderstands the most basic terms in the thought of Zarathustra so badly that, given his level of intellect, one has to conclude that this is one of those many cases of an intellectual who should know better than to engage in incoherent discourse on account of deeply rooted religious convictions that he is unwilling to question. There have been many such examples, from medieval European Christian scholastics such as Saint Augustine and Thomas Aquinas to Iranian thinkers like Al-Farabi and Al-Biruni, whose otherwise formidable minds were equally diseased by their pathetic faith in Islam.

Steiner is another one who is compelled by his faith in Christ to engage in grotesque mental gymnastics. Steiner separates Lucifer from Ahriman, and then introduces Jesus Christ as a mediating figure and savior of mankind between the two. According to Steiner, Lucifer is a transcendent power that pulls those humans connected with him up beyond the sensory sphere of earthly life into an angelic realm of abstract principles and sublime intuitions. Meanwhile, Ahriman is a demonic power that tries to draw mankind down into an earthly or "chthonic" experience of pure materialism that would close off human access to the divine reality that is above and beyond man. The Redeemer Christ, whose crucifixion as Jesus at Golgotha Steiner sees as the most important and salvific event in human history, is a mediator who can save mankind from being torn apart by these two forces, allowing people to remain grounded enough so as to choose to align themselves with the divine and thereby unfold their God-given potential. Steiner claims that this tripartite scheme was already intended by Zarathustra, who was the chief Magi or Magus of a Sun Oracle that is proto-Christian in nature such that, going all the way back to Atlantis, the eventual coming of Christ as the Redeemer was awaited and known to be the culminating event of human history.

This could not be further from the actual teaching of Zarathustra. "Ahriman" is a Middle Persian contraction of *Angra Mainyu*, the more ancient Iranian term that Zarathustra actually uses. It means "mentality of constriction or constraint." In the *Gathas* of Zarathustra, this term appears as part of a polarity that includes *Spenta Mainyu*, or the "progressive and bounteous mentality." *Spenta Mainyu* is the principal attribute of *Ahura Mazda* or the "titan of Wisdom." *Ahura* is the ancient Iranian cognate of the Sanskrit *Ashura*, which as indicated above is the Hindu name of the titans who rebelled against the gods—such as Prometheus and Atlas. Prometheus as the rebel titan who brings the forbidden wisdom to mortals is doing so for the sake of catalyzing the progressive innovation characteristic of *Spenta Mainyu*. What he is opposing is the constriction or constraint, and consequently, the stagnation or stasis, of the divinely ordained society of oppressed mortals into which he is bringing this disruptive fire. In the *Gathas*, Zarathustra literally refers to the Devas or Olympian gods as deluded deceivers who came together in a congress or council meeting at which they deliberated to the end of "rushing into the earthly world to destroy the life of mankind." This is Zarathustra's way of describing the convocation of the gods that Plato refers to at the end of *Critias*, the meeting called by Zeus (the Deva Indra) to decide on destroying Atlantis with the global deluge. In other words, the "flood of Noah" that, we are told in Genesis, the Father of Jesus Christ came to believe was necessary to wipe the Earth clean of what the rebellious hybrids had done with the secret knowledge gifted to them by the Fallen Angels. All of which is to say that any decent theologian should recognize that Zarathustra's teaching is a 180-degree inversion of the Indo-European theology, wherein the titanic rebellion is valorized, and the Devas or gods are the ones demonized as the avatars of Ahriman.

Furthermore, there is no metaphysical dualism of the kind that is rife in the worldview of Steiner, or for that matter, implicitly, in Edgar Cayce's account of Atlantis as well. It was not until the era of Mani, in the third century AD, many hundreds of years after the time of Zarathustra (probably, despite Steiner's claims for a much older date, circa 600 BC), that dualism became a prominent feature of certain

Gnostic currents in Persian religion. In the *Gathas* of Zarathustra, the earthly realm is seen as a wonderful and potentially joy-bringing creation that ought to be artificially engineered and augmented by human innovation so as to turn it into a paradise (the word "paradise" literally comes from the ancient Persian *pari-daeza*, or "fairy garden"). Human beings themselves are supposed to achieve a more perfect, superhuman state of embodiment through aligning themselves with the Spirit of Innovation or the Progressive Mentality, such that after an apocalyptic end of merely human history, known as the *Frashgard*, they will become *frashtes*, or fiery superhuman beings free from the frailties of the mortal coil. Interestingly, such beings of fire are the same entities referred to as Jinn by the Arabs, and that, as we saw in the previous chapter, Traditionalists in the vein of Guénon want to believe were the antediluvian demonic race who is still seducing mankind through the Close Encounter phenomenon. Anyway, not to get sidetracked, the point is that from Zarathustra's perspective, it is the Children of the Law of One who are Ahrimanic, and the Belial group embody the principal attribute of Ahura Mazda—who is essentially a less anthropomorphic and more abstract idea of Prometheus. Steiner's separation of the Luciferian from the Ahrimanic is, whether he realized it or not, an Olympian psychological warfare tactic of divide and conquer.

Edgar Cayce, independently and unconsciously, agrees with Rudolf Steiner in characterizing the Belial group as "materialists." But by the logic of Cayce's own narrative, or for that matter even Steiner's account, that cannot possibly be true. The point that Cayce makes over and over again in his Atlantis readings is that the very same science and technology that the Children of the Law of One used for putatively proper divine purposes—which Steiner calls "spiritual science"—were supposedly being profaned and perverted for secular purposes by the Belial group. Steiner calls this the perversion of the secret knowledge of the Mysteries, or what is really a use of them that renders them no longer "mysterious." So, in addition to all of the practical arts and crafts mentioned in the Book of Enoch and paralleled in the myth of the gift of *techne* to mankind by Prometheus, everything that we would today associate with magic or sorcery is also included.

The Belial group were not only using aetheric energy to propel their aircraft and submarines or using crystals to build death rays and the like, or employing genetic engineering to design transhuman chimera, or cybernetically creating a race of automatons, they were just as readily employing telepathy, clairvoyance, precognition, and telekinesis for worldly purposes. This stripped these phenomena of any veneer of miraculous or mysterious association with some supposedly divine order above or beyond us, recognizing instead that these are latent and trainable abilities that we can cultivate to a level comparable to the "super powers" of those who would set themselves up as gods above us. This is the real "sin" of the Belial group. They treated Parapsychology or Psychotronics just as they treated Physics, Engineering, and Genetics.

The Belial group in Atlantis were most certainly not materialists; they just rejected the metaphysically dualistic theology used by the "Law of One" cult to justify the continued tyranny of the gods over the Earth. A tyranny disguised as a beneficent consciousness-raising plan to redeem spiritual beings from their fall into a material realm. Only a dualist would say that the Belial group were materialists. The proper characterization would be something like "spectral empiricists." They must have rejected the entire metaphysically dualist account of human origins that was part of the Law of One or Mystery School theology as affirmatively recounted by Cayce and Steiner. The rebel Atlanteans' own view of human origins is as thoroughly effaced in these heresiologies as if we were to read about a group of Darwinists in textbooks penned by Creationists in some post-apocalyptic and post-industrial dystopia, wherein scientific empiricism, including (and especially) Parapsychology, has been retrospectively branded as "that wicked hubris that brought about the end of the old world."

This brings us to the fifth and final element common to all of the accounts of Atlantis, which is the cause of the super-civilization's destruction. By cause here I do not necessarily mean the physical cause of the demise of Atlantis, which the various sources differ on. Rather, I mean the root cause, which every source agrees had to do with the Atlantean rebellion against the gods and the world order that they had established. Plato claims that Atlantis was "destroyed in a night and a day" by earthquakes and flooding in 9600 BC. According to Steiner, the date was precisely 9564 BC, and the earthquakes and flooding did not have a purely physical cause but was triggered by a psychic war that had erupted within the society between its two principal factions, each turning their telekinetic powers on one another, bringing destruction through the psychotronic manipulation of natural forces. According to Edgar Cayce, there were three destructions of Atlantis, over a span of tens of thousands of years. The first was around 50,000 BC when the first seismic disturbances occurred. The second destruction, around 28,000 BC, was more severe and also seismic in nature, shattering the island continent into a chain of smaller islands, the largest of which was named Poseidea. According to Cayce, Plato was referring only to the final destruction of Atlantis, as a consequence of the supposed misuse of technology by the Sons of Belial in their conflict with the Children of the Law of One, circa 10,000 BC. In one way or another, all of them agree that whatever the specific cause of the final destruction, its ultimate cause was the rebellion of the irreverent faction against the putatively divine order. Even in Steiner, one of the two sides in the psychic war are the Atlanteans who remain aligned with Olympus and are representatives of the gods.

One of the most fundamental points of contention between these two warring factions of Atlanteans seems to have been the question of what to do with the "things." We get the clearest account of this from Edgar Cayce. The "things" were essentially humanoid robots or biomechanical androids, created by means of genetic engineering and cybernetics. To call them "slaves" would be to overestimate their degree of consciousness and sense of agency. These entities were employed in every form of labor and diversion, thereby providing a life of luxury and convenience for the Atlanteans. If we were to believe the narrative of Cayce, the Christian Sunday school teacher, the Children of the Law of One wanted to raise the consciousness of these beings by bringing them into the aforementioned "initiatory hierarchy," read caste system, that promised them eventual spiritual salvation through successive reincarnations wherein their lives would be devoted to service (as a means to supposed "spiritual purification"). Whereas the Belial group considered these "things" to be soulless and wanted to keep them soulless, or lacking consciousness, so that they could perform the tasks for which they were designed.

These divergent views of the "things" are based on the more fundamental clash of worldviews between the two groups of Atlanteans. Again, we are left to reconstruct the view of the Belial group based on what is essentially heresiology favorable to the Children of the Law of One. Since the latter subscribed to a dualistic metaphysics, and a scheme of spiritual salvation from a fallen material world through faith in the One True God, they could argue that all legitimate "creative force"—as Cayce calls it—belongs to this God, and that the "things" are like other fallen souls, just even more mired in matter. One can think of this in terms of the Hindu theology of *atman* and *Brahman* that, according to Steiner, was eventually derived from the earlier Atlantean prototype. Anything humanoid must have some kind of *atman*, however ensnared by the delusory veil of *maya* (the illusion of the material world). By contrast, the Belial group had, in some regards, a view that, at least on an ontological and epistemological level, if not on an ethical one, was a precursor to the atheism of Gautama Buddha, who argued that there was neither an *atman* nor was there *Brahman*. The Buddha thought that these were sophisticated and self-deluding projections. Likewise, according to the Belial group, there was no existing indestructible core of personhood that would be a microcosm of the macrocosm of God and thereby subject to some supposed cosmic Law of One (*karma* and *dharma*). Whereas the consciousness and memories of a conscious and individuated person could be transferred from one body to another, the way that software is transferred from one piece of hardware to another, a being lacking in consciousness and individuated identity is a thing and not a person. The best analogy for understanding this is the distinction between avatars of gamers and Non-Player Characters (NPCs) in the multiplayer role-playing games of our Cyberspace.

If we were to put ourselves into the perspective of the Belial group, and to reason together with them about the "things," we would see that they considered the moralizing of the Children of the Law of One to be deeply dishonest, if not outright duplicitous. These Traditionalist Theists wanted to treat the "things" as souls in need of salvation because to acknowledge that they were no such things would destroy their entire system of belief and the caste hierarchy that ensured human subservience to the gods. What they really wanted to do was to entangle the "things" in their pyramid scheme. To admit that the automatons were just that, a race of robots that afforded human individuals the luxury and leisure to live self-directed lives free from demeaning drudgery, would be a fatal blow to human subservience to the gods and the Mystery Schools organized around these "mysterious" divine beings. To treat the "things" *as things* would, in effect, mean that humans—or rather, the hybrid demigod population of Atlantis—would become a godlike race with its own self-determined sphere of worldly purposes, aims, and ambitions, with no regard whatsoever for any gods above or beyond themselves, unbound to any supposed divine law decreed by these Overlords. In other words, they would be *Beli-el, Beli-ya'al, Beli-ol*—godless, lawless, and unbound. We are essentially talking about a group of parapsychologically adept, transhumanist, atheistic and anarchic existentialists who are resisting Theistic Traditionalism. They believe neither in God nor in an indestructible soul, and they want their robots to be robots.

Granted, the technology for engineering the "things" seems to have been more genetic and cybernetic than purely mechanical, but biological robots are still robots. The Atlanteans were so adept at genetic engineering that they managed to bring the dinosaurs back from extinction. Cayce recounts a *Jurassic Park*-type scenario, wherein these dinosaurs, including and especially flying dinosaurs or "dragons," got out of hand and threatened the safety and security of the Atlantean city dwellers. With peculiar precision he tells us that in the year 50,722 BC there was a worldwide television broadcast by a think tank, whose members traveled by airship to a central location where they devised a plan for the elimination of these gigantic beasts. (It was misuse of the technology developed for this purpose that led to the first of the three destructions recounted by Cayce.) In any case, presumably by means of the same gene-splicing techniques used to bring the dinosaurs back, the "mad scientists" of the Belial group had turned some of the "things" into human-animal hybrids or chimeras of various sorts: humanoids with horns, hooves, tails, or wings. Cayce claims that this was as much to show off, on the part of the designers and owners of these chimerical things, as it was for any practical purpose, such as conferring some of the abilities of a certain nonhuman animal to an automaton that would consequently perform its designated task more effectively.

Despite Edgar Cayce's proven track record as an adept psychic and medium (which cannot be denied no matter how much I despise him for his religious beliefs), I would still be inclined to treat much of this narrative as fantastical—were it not the case that, as I discussed in Chapter 2, I also have fragmentary memories of this lost world. These are the fragments that I embroidered in order to develop the depiction of Atlantis in *Faustian Futurist*. The fragments themselves are, well, fragmentary, and have remained entirely consistent. They came to me spontaneously at several different points in my life. On the one occasion that I attempted past life regression hypnosis in order to excavate a broader context for these memories and attain a more high-fidelity recollection of my apparent past life (or lives) in Atlantis, the woman turned out to be an incompetent hypnotist and a charlatan, who was trying to implant false memories into my mind by repeatedly prompting me to imaginatively spin a yarn from out of my authentic bits of memory. I walked out of the session and never attempted it again.

As someone with a very active imagination, the phenomenological difference between imagination and recollection is perfectly clear to me. The experiential quality of the one is completely different from that of the other. Just think back to fragmentary childhood memories, unaided by, but sometimes corroborated by, one or another photograph. That kind of experience is totally different from making up a story. Now it is possible to have false memories of "experiences" in childhood that are not accurate recollections of any actual events that took place, but that is a rare psychological condition often overemphasized by those with a vested interest in dismissing the memories of certain people who recollect traumatic abuse in childhood. Furthermore, having analyzed the late Dr. Ian Stevenson's vast database of empirical research on children's experiences of reincarnation, I have no reason to doubt that my memories of any one or another past life are any more unconsciously confabulated than the many cases that Stevenson and his colleagues at the University of Virginia rigorously studied.

As in the case of my memories of having been Nikola Tesla, my past life recollections of Atlantis, which I have recounted in Chapter 2, first surfaced in early childhood and then a flood of memories came to me around the time that I met "Emma" (who, as I explained, had memories that interlocked with mine). The resurfacing of these memories of Atlantis prompted me to thoroughly research the subject. I remember being captivated by the pictures of high-precision megalithic stonework in books like Graham Hancock's *Fingerprints of the Gods*. From the walls of Sacsayhuaman to those of Ollantaytambo in the Andes to the Sphinx and Valley Temples in Egypt, the style struck me as uncannily familiar: the jigsaw pattern of the interlocking blocks, their precision and impossible scale, the way that some of them even smoothly rounded the corners of buildings. It was all as "native" to me as it was utterly alien to anything that any of the historically known civilizations ought to have been capable of achieving with the tools and knowledge at their disposal. The Kalasasaya at Tiwanaku and the Osireion at Abydos both seemed so recognizable to me that I could swear I had been to both structures, or to someplace very much like them but prior to their being in a ruined condition.

On that note, they also reminded me of Brutalist architecture, to which I had a strange connection as a style that I did not necessarily "like" at all (I am most partial to Art Deco and Art Nouveau) but that I felt terribly at home with. I got the sense that structures like the Kalasasaya and the Osireion, much like the similarly austere and unadorned interior chambers and walkways of the Great Pyramid at Giza, had originally been more Brutalist in style or were modeled on something that was. Something as futuristic as it was archaic. Something inhuman in both style and scale. Although I also had an intuition—or perhaps even a recollection—that flowing water was often geometrically engineered into these structures in a way that somewhat softened their titanic brutality.

Another thing that I remember, or was reminded of, by the research of the Belgian engineer Robert Bauval in particular, was that many of the Atlantean structures were designed as an earthly microcosmic representation of macrocosmic astronomical configurations and astrological constellations. This fits the worldview of the old guard that Cayce calls "the Children of the Law of One." There was a great deal of astrological determinism in their ideology, down to the precise planning of conception and birth according to the Zodiacal calendar and a degree of deference to stellar and planetary influences that bordered on oppressive fatalism. The alignments that Bauval discovered in the ground plan of the Giza structures, wherein the pyramids reflect the three stars of Orion's belt, the Nile River mirrors the Milky Way, and the Sphinx gazes at its counterpart, the constellation of Leo, just before dawn on the Spring Equinox around 10,500

BC, is a building principle that the Atlantean establishment adhered to even more conservatively than the ancient Chinese arranged structures and spaces according to Feng Shui—which, by the way, was also Atlantean in origin. Robert Schoch's redating of the Sphinx based on a geological assessment of the degree of water-based erosion that it has sustained (together with the two temples that were built from out of the stone loosed by carving the monument out of its trench), has gone a long way in validating Cayce's claim that the Atlanteans themselves constructed the Giza structures—possibly even before the final destruction of Atlantis (renovating them thereafter). These austerely unmarked structures, which lack *any* hieroglyphics or bas reliefs, are certainly not characteristic of anything commissioned by a megalomaniacal Egyptian Pharaoh who never hesitated to (sometimes repeatedly) take credit for whatever he had built.

The only thing that really confused me in those early years of obsessive research on Atlantis was the location of the civilization. Or, rather, I should say of the Atlantean homeland. It was clear that even before the exodus of Atlanteans to various parts of the world—South America, Egypt, India, the Gobi, etc.—after the final destruction, they had a largely maritime worldwide empire. Plato's account in *Critias* centers on the Atlantean naval invasion and attempted colonization of the Mediterranean coastlines, including antediluvian Greece. So, the refugees fled to preexisting colonies all over the world. But there remains the question of the homeland. Where was it? This is something that, quite honestly, I do not remember and cannot piece together from my fragmentary memories. I have no bird's eye view, as it were, of the landmass in relation to other geographical regions.

What I do know is that, as Plato accurately described, Atlantis was vast. He describes an island continent, or a number of closely connected islands (including one very large one), that covers an area comparable to the Achaemenid Persian Empire of his era or the continental United States today. He was also right that there were snow-capped mountains in Atlantis that were of a scale comparable to the

Rockies or the Himalayas. For those reasons I have been partial to the idea first proposed by Rand Flem-Ath, based on the Earth Crustal Displacement theory of Professor Charles Hapgood, that a partially ice-free Antarctica was Atlantis (before being catastrophically pulled several thousand miles deeper into the southern polar region). This theory was later adopted and expanded upon by Colin Wilson, for whom I have always had great respect, not just as a researcher, but as a penetrating philosophical thinker. (Wilson died just after I requested that he write a foreword to *Prometheus and Atlas*—the first of my books wherein I engage with the subject of Atlantis.) Finally, Plato did not say that Atlantis was right outside the "Pillars of Hercules" or the Strait of Gibraltar. He wrote that it was somewhere beyond the Strait of Gibraltar in the "world ocean" and that from the huge island continent the opposite side of the world could be easily reached. There is one place on Earth where we really have a "world ocean." In the waters around Antarctica, the Atlantic, Indian, and Pacific Oceans become a single ocean, and by traversing Antarctica, or navigating around its coastline, one can readily cross over from the Eastern to the Western hemisphere of Earth.

However, this is one of the subjects of my writings that I continue to harbor the most doubt about. It is entirely possible that Atlantis was some catastrophically sunken landmass that once existed in the North Atlantic Ocean, as Senator Ignatius Donnelly hypothesized in his classic study on the subject. Edgar Cayce may have been right that the largest island of Atlantis, namely Poseidea, was in that part of the North Atlantic that is now the Bahamas and the Caribbean, in particular somewhere between Bermuda, Bimini, Puerto Rico, Cuba, and the part of the Yucatán Peninsula that juts into the Gulf of Mexico. One of the biggest pieces of evidence in favor of this hypothesis is the Bermuda Triangle, also formerly known as the Sargasso Sea, a veritable death trap of paranormal phenomena that has caused the disappearance—and transitory ghostly reappearance—of many ships and aircraft in the area. Some ship captains and crew, and certain airplane pilots, have even briefly seen huge landmasses appear and then suddenly disappear again within the Bermuda Triangle. Undoubtedly, the place features some kind of spatiotemporal vortex, which may be caused by the electromagnetic force of Atlantean energy technology of the kind that Cayce describes. Compasses have been known to turn backwards in certain parts of the Sargasso Sea. Then, there is the matter of the sunken ruins—the many massive megalithic ruins that are being hidden in the Caribbean and Bahamas Basins. This area, especially around Puerto Rico and Cuba, is also a hotbed for USOs or UFOs that are seen entering and exiting the ocean, prompting much speculation about undersea Atlantean bases.

In 1968, several divers off the coast of Bimini (Joseph Manson Valentine, Jacques Mayol, and Robert Angove) discovered megalithic engineering, more or less as Edgar Cayce had predicted back in the 1930s and 40s. The "sleeping prophet" had said that this was the first place where "around '68" Atlantis would begin to be rediscovered. This structure is a half-mile (0.8 kilometers) long top of a "wall," or the pavement of a "road" built of roughly rectangular limestone blocks. It is situated at a depth of 18 feet (5.5 meters) below the surface of the ocean.

This is nothing to compare with what a team led by Paulina Zelitsky discovered on the Guanahacabibes Peninsula off the western tip of Cuba in 2001. On the first expedition, in January, sonar-scanning equipment discovered no less than two square miles of massive geometric structures that appeared to be man-made. Returning in July, Zelitsky and her fellow researchers sent an exploratory robot armed with cameras to dive on the structures. What they found was a megalithic city built of smooth granite blocks, featuring several very large pyramids and other polygonal buildings of a titanic scale. The buildings are at a depth of 2,000 feet or 650 meters beneath the surface, which means that they could not have been submerged by gradual sea level rise, even over the course of ten thousand or more years. Global sea levels have only risen by about 300 feet since the end of the ice age. In other words, this is a *sunken* city. It must have precipitously sunk, all in one piece, to where it now lays on the ocean floor. This lends credence to Cayce's otherwise incredible claim that Atlantis, as a landmass, literally sank rather than simply being flooded.

After news reports came out in the BBC and other mainstream media outlets, oceanographic researchers at the level of National Geographic promised to investigate the deeply disturbing find. Now, more than twenty years later, no further research has been done and the astonishing find has been all but forgotten. Rather, it has been made to be forgotten and put out of the public mind.

Paulina Zelitsky was brutally intimidated from further investigating the site herself, having been thrown in a Mexican prison during her investigation of the site's possible connection to ruins in the Yucatan. When diving on the site, Zelitsky claimed that she saw hieroglyphics on the structures, which reminded her of Mayan writing. Suffice it to say, she returned to Canada and never came back to continue uncovering Atlantis.

CHAPTER 5

DE PROFUNDIS EXCELSIOR

THERE IS ANOTHER woman who, as an expert diver, a submarine captain, and helicopter pilot, has used her extensive connections to the global elite to go to even greater lengths than Zelitsky to rediscover Atlantis. However, between her own clearly justified discretion, and the defamation by omission that she has now suffered at the hands of the mainstream media — which are obviously being manipulated to literally keep Atlantis buried or, as it were, submerged — one would never know that an Atlantean Renaissance was her secret life's quest. That extraordinary woman is Ghislaine Maxwell. What follows is the story behind the story of my having written Ghislaine into such a prominent role in *Uber Man*, as the lover and life partner of Dana Avalon, the novel's protagonist, and as the leader of AtlantiCorp's "NovAtlantis" project.

"New Atlantis" (of which NovAtlantis is a Latinate contraction) was the name of a project launched by Leicester Hemingway in 1964 to build a micronation off the coast of Jamaica in the Caribbean Sea. Leicester, the younger brother of author Ernest Hemingway, was a follower of Edgar Cayce's claims that the currently submerged landmass of Atlantis would literally rise again in this area. For his part, Ernest

Hemingway spent many years in the Caribbean, living both on the coast of Cuba and also at Bimini. He wrote *The Old Man and the Sea* (1952) here. He was sighted crisscrossing the sea in a boat strangely full of scientific equipment. While Hemingway claimed to be looking for German U-boats, the truth is probably that he had already sighted what was "discovered" only decades later off the coasts of Bimini and Cuba, and that he was searching for Atlantis.

Both Hemingway brothers supposedly committed suicide. But before meeting their demise, they struck up a friendship with the famous ocean explorer Jacques Cousteau. After his father's death, Jacques' son, Philippe Cousteau, claimed that despite the carefully cultivated public image, his father was far less concerned about ocean conservation than he was about finding Atlantis, which, according to Philippe, had really been Jacques Cousteau's lifelong quest. Phillipe Cousteau went on to investigate Atlantis himself, producing a notable documentary film on his research together with David Zink, author of *The Stones of Atlantis*. Very shortly after the production of that documentary, titled *Calypso's Search for Atlantis* (1993), Philippe Cousteau died an untimely death, at the age of only 38, in a supposed airplane accident.

Ghislaine Maxwell has gone on the record about how, from childhood when she would watch his television programs with fascination, Jacques Cousteau inspired her lifelong love of ocean exploration. According to Virginia Giuffre's testimony, Ghislaine had an erotic relationship with Philippe Cousteau's daughter — in other words, Jacques Cousteau's granddaughter — marine activist Alexandra Cousteau. Jeffrey Epstein gave a significant donation to the Cousteau Society.

Ghislaine took up diving by the age of nine and was an expert before reaching adulthood. I imagine that by this time she was already fascinated by Atlantis, perhaps having watched, at some point in her childhood, *Atlantis, the Lost Continent*, an epic Hollywood film that premiered in 1961, the year of her birth. I could easily see how a young Ghislaine might have identified with Princess Antillia in the film about a Greek fisherman who is taken aboard an Atlantean submarine and has to fight his way out of slavery in Atlantis on the eve of the planned Atlantean invasion of the Mediterranean. The interest sparked (or anamnetically rekindled) by that movie might have led her to the book *Atlantis Rising* by Brad Steiger, a work published in 1973 when she was 12. The work summarized every major theory about Atlantis, pointing the reader to all of the other studies that had been done ever since serious research on the subject was spearheaded by Senator Ignatius Donnelly in his *Atlantis: The Antediluvian World* (1882). Then, beginning in September of 1977, when she was 15, the American television series *The Man from Atlantis* aired in the United Kingdom, even beating *Doctor Who* for popularity amongst British sci-fi fans. The pilot episode is about a mad scientist who tries to set up a breakaway civilization inside of a hollowed-out mountain at the bottom of the ocean, from where he aims to trigger a nuclear war on the surface world so that the oceans can be protected from further degradation and destruction at the hands of mankind. He also plans to artificially evolve a posthuman aquatic race. Marvel comics briefly serialized the show in 1978, so that its protagonist, Mark Harris, became the third comic book hero from Atlantis in the popular culture of the time, joining Marvel's own Submariner and DC's Aquaman. I have no doubt that in the 1990s she was watching Roy Scheider play the lead role in the sci-fi show *seaQuest DSV*.

Ghislaine eventually trained to become both a submarine pilot and a helicopter pilot. The submarine that she piloted during her expeditions in the Caribbean with Jeffrey Epstein and company was named "Atlantis." Ghislaine Maxwell adopted the pseudonym "Janet Atlantis" to acquire property in New Hampshire as a fugitive from the so-called "Justice" system that turned the cell cameras off and sent the prison guards away while Epstein was assassinated in a maximum-security federal facility on August 10 of 2019. She may have been inspired to do so by having read the works of Janet Atlantis Marshall or Janet Stevenson, a feminist author who wrote a gripping novel of the sea, *Departure*, about a female ship's captain struggling to command a crew of tough-minded men who might mutiny against her. But JANET is also a military-intelligence acronym that means Just Another Non-Existent Terminal. It is used to designate the secret airports that private jets of the Black Ops world fly in and out of, private planes like the one she often rode on with Epstein. But there is more to the joke. After all, Ms. Maxwell is known to have a wicked sense of humor. With her interest in the Buddhist philosophical idea of no-self (*anatta*), and her extensive connections to intelligence agencies, both through Jeffrey Epstein and even more so, on account of her father's work as a super-spy and triple agent, I believe that Ghislaine also had this meaning in mind when she assumed the name "Janet Atlantis."

"Robert Maxwell" was probably one of the most important intelligence operatives of the 20th century. I put his name in quotes because, of course, it was not the one he was born with. Rather it was one of a series of pseudonyms and operational identities, the one that eventually stuck and upon which he built a life in the public eye. Ján Ludvik Hyman Binyamin Hoch was born in 1923, in what was then Slatinské Doly, Czechoslovakia, and is now Solotvyno, Ukraine. (Yes, Ukraine.) Most of his family was killed in the Holocaust, specifically at Auschwitz. Hoch joined the Czechoslovak army division of the French Resistance in World War II. Then, using the names "Ivan du Maurier" or "Leslie du Maurier" (after the popular Maurier cigarette brand), he distinguished himself for heroism and shrewd tactics in the struggle against Nazi Germany, such that he was able to work his way into British Military Intelligence at the rank of captain. At this point, he spoke at least four languages.

As he built a career in the publishing industry in the 1950s under the new assumed name of Robert Maxwell, using Allied wartime connections, Hoch secretly became a spy for the KGB. In other words, he was a double agent for the United Kingdom (specifically for MI6) and the Soviet Union. Then, sometime after the birth of Ghislaine in Paris, in 1961, Maxwell reconnected with his Jewish roots and as a high-level operative for the Mossad he became a triple agent. When he was buried in Jerusalem in November of 1991, at a state funeral attended by several former and future Israeli heads of state, then Prime Minister Yitzhak Shamir said, in his eulogy, that Robert Maxwell "has done more for Israel than can today be told."

Everyone knew that Ghislaine was the favorite from among his nine children, the "daddy's girl" after whom he named the ill-fated yacht, the *Lady Ghislaine*, from which he disappeared in the middle of the night on November 5, 1991, as the ship cruised off the coasts of the Canary Islands. When his naked body was recovered from the ocean and brought back to Las Palmas, Ghislaine refused to believe that he had committed suicide or even been the victim of an accidental drowning. If anyone would have known who was out to get him and why, it would have been her.

"Captain Bob," as he was called aboard the *Lady Ghislaine*, had extensive international corporate, political, and elite social connections (including to the British royal family), some of which were forged by Ghislaine herself in her capacity as his de facto executive secretary and socialite connector, and some of which she built upon, and expanded beyond, after his death. It was this network that Jeffrey Epstein wanted from Ghislaine following the precipitous destruction of the Maxwell business empire on account of fraud charges, which, as Ghislaine put it, left her "broke." Robert Maxwell had met Jeffrey Epstein in the mid to late 1980s (when Epstein was already a "money manager" for billionaires like Les Wexner). Maxwell traveled to Israel with Epstein and recruited him to work for the Mossad as a financier, arms dealer, bounty hunter, and blackmailer. Ghislaine appears to have met Epstein through her father, sometime shortly before his death. But I wager that it is only after Epstein got involved with Ghislaine, following her move to Manhattan in early 1992, that he developed rather esoteric interests connected to the Atlantis mythos in one way or another.

For example, when Epstein bought Little St. James in 1998, he built an Atlantean temple on the far end of the island, adorned with idols of Poseidon and Atlas. Meanwhile, at his Zorro ranch, Epstein had a labyrinthine circular garden designed and planted in the unmistakable form of the ground plan of the city of Atlantis, with its cross and concentric rings, as provided by Plato in *Critias*. Then there is the story that leaked out about how Epstein was planning a Eugenics project at the ranch, wherein the eugenically selected for "models" that he was collecting would be surrogates for genetically enhanced children engineered, in part, with his own sperm. Granted, Epstein might have gotten the idea from OSS agent Donald Barr's salacious sci-fi novel *Space Relations* (1973), sometime after Barr hired him to teach math at the Dalton School, where Barr had become the headmaster. But could this Eugenics project actually have had more to do with what the Belial group was up to in Atlantis? If Ghislaine was significantly involved in soliciting these "models," was it really simply to satisfy Epstein's enormous sexual appetite, or even to set up prominent politicians with underage women so as to blackmail them? Why is it that most of them were Nordic-looking?

Why did Ghislaine hire a series of blond-haired and blue-eyed Swedish young men to be her low-level personal assistants when she lived, from 2000 to 2019, in her townhouse at 116 East 65th Street? She *only* hired these types, and she brought them from Sweden on tourist visas, rotating these live-ins every three months. Ghislaine told one of them that she had never even been to Sweden. He also said that Ghislaine kept a grenade on her office desk at all times and was very concerned (I would not say paranoid, at least not without cause) that she could be assassinated by someone who could gain unauthorized access to the house. (The grenade reminds me of the cover of *The Invisibles*.) Were strands of hair and other genetic material being collected from the basement room occupied by these live-in Swedish assistants, apropos of the film *Gattaca*?

Could the Nordic phenotype of most of Epstein's women and of Ghislaine's male assistants have had anything to do with the various racial theories surrounding Atlantis and the "master race" since the days of Blavatsky and the Thule Society? Anyone who balks at this thought by citing the fact that Ghislaine is Jewish by birth, and that her grandparents were killed in the Holocaust, or that both she and her father worked with the Mossad, forget that Otto Skorzeny, the head of the Spider (aka ODESSA) worked with the Mossad as well and was very helpful to the State of Israel in the last decade of his life. The dynamics of the world we live in are very dialectically complex.

By the way, the one Epstein girl that I knew was also Nordic in appearance. That is quite astonishing actually, considering the fact that the Dalton School was at that time something like 70% Jewish in its demographic, and the remaining 30% mostly consisted of various minority groups, including a decent number of Asians. Gentile blonde bombshells were a rare species at my high school. The first I heard of her extracurricular activities was when she confided that she was doing teenage modeling for Victoria's Secret. This girl was, shall we say, sexually precocious. She did some overtime in the headmaster's office and I am sure it has nothing to do with the fact that she managed to get into Harvard despite not exactly being the bookish type. (I am not judging, by the way, although that particular headmaster made my skin crawl.) Then again, it was probably Epstein who got her into Harvard with the substantive donations that he gave to that university. (Epstein had keycard access to an office at the Evolutionary Dynamics program at Harvard until 2018, even after he had already been arrested and prosecuted for the first time in 2006.) Eventually, this blonde (I have it on good authority that she was a *natural* blonde) became a successful model and actress. (How many other women that Epstein solicited knew *exactly* what they were doing, and would never be driven by resentment to retroactively protest because they benefited greatly from their early life career investment?) Anyway, this was one of the times that I almost met Ghislaine Maxwell, around 1996.

I might add that you should take a look at my Dalton School yearbook from 1995. My middle school graduation picture is me at the age of 14, *wearing a suit* with dark glasses and standing before an old tank in front of the headquarters of British Intelligence in London. The quote, which, as much as the picture, stands out from every other one accompanying the childish photos of my peers, is *not* a quote. It is a statement from myself: "Information is the greatest weapon." In a list of remarks describing each member of the eighth-grade graduating class, which classmates came up with for one another, and most of which are totally innocuous and benignly humorous, the one that my peers wrote for me speaks volumes about who I already was in 1995, at age 14. The general header for the page reads "8th Grade Wouldn't Be The Same If..." and my entry is "...Jason Jorjani couldn't access the White House, the CIA..."

What kernel of truth was this colorful line based on? We had a history professor named Cameron Hendershot, who was a recruiter for the CIA. He taught me in the seventh grade, and based on his experience with me, he was already trying to recruit me by the eighth grade. Hendershot would share low classification reports on US strategic assessments of Iranian military capabilities with me to help with a 60-page report that I wrote for Social Studies in 1995, titled "The Coming Iranian Superpower." My teacher (the one who warned me that Hendershot was a CIA recruiter) reacted to my report by saying, "I asked for a 20-page term paper, not a dissertation." Hendershot's wife was positioned as the head librarian of the Dalton library, thereby keeping tabs on what students took out which books.

The Epstein girl that I mentioned wrote the following inscription in my yearbook that year: "Jason, Hi! I'm happy you wrote me that letter, too. Can't wait 'till next year... maybe we'll be in the same house (I hear they put a smart kid with a dumb one). Thanks for not being superficial, and striving to see the real me. I'll always appreciate that. Love, ..." I was friendly with this girl, and I became concerned for her welfare after seeing her get picked up at Dalton by a man with greyish hair (more salt in it than pepper), wearing a black leather jacket and blue jeans. What I did not know at the time was that he was Jeffrey Epstein.

When I ran into him inside the black metal bars of the gate outside the front entrance, he said to me, almost apologetically (averting his gaze from mine, with his eyes looking down and to the side), "I used to teach here," as if it were meant to be some explanatory justification for why he was taking *her* away with him. (I carried this girl across a beach in my arms once.) I was of a mind to pry into who he was and prod my way into her secret life when dramatic events (that I now believe to have been engineered) unfolded, which distracted me and made me lose interest in going to the trouble to do so. Had that not happened, I would likely have met Ghislaine Maxwell by 1997. I probably did see her, but there is something to inverting the old saying, "out of sight, out of mind." If something, or someone, can be put out of mind, she can also be put out of sight. "Out of mind, out of sight" is the principle that is used by the Breakaway Civilization to ensure that no one in the surface world reincarnates in any of their undersea or lunar colonies. No one would know to even look for such places while traversing the bardo state after death.

By the way, Ghislaine Maxwell has always been into the occult. She is a fan of *Twin Peaks* and other David Lynch productions; she loves ghost stories, and her favorite holiday is Halloween. Epstein was also into the paranormal, once threatening journalist Vicky Ward that he had access to practitioners of voodoo that could cause her to miscarry if she portrayed him in a negative light in an article that she was writing. Ward wound up having serious complications with her pregnancy. When being held at the Brooklyn Metropolitan Detention Center, Ghislaine started making strange statements about her "imaginary friend," with whom she would have conversations, a poltergeist or an egregore that was psychokinetically interacting with her environment and that apparently scared the prison guards. She named the entity "A-17." Q is the 17th letter of the alphabet, and ".aq" is the domain address for the select few people who live or work in Antarctica.

Ghislaine Maxwell and I were probably at the same place, at the same time, on the Upper East Side, on at least half a dozen occasions, including at the reception for my graduation from Dalton in June of 1999, which was held at the Frick, literally around the corner from Epstein's townhouse at 71st street off Fifth Avenue—most ironically, the site of the former Imperial Iranian consulate to the United Nations—where Ghislaine was living at the time before she got her own townhouse a few blocks further south. Congratulations would certainly have been in order for this one model and classmate of mine. This alone would have justified Ghislaine's presence there that evening. Lucifer only knows how many other times our paths crossed, for example, at high-end Park Avenue Armory art shows (that I really had no business being at in my early twenties) a couple of blocks from the townhouse at 65th street that she moved into in 2000. This much I can say for certain. I have always had excellent visual memory, and facial recognition in particular. Ghislaine Maxwell looks uncannily familiar to me, especially in photographs that were taken in her forties. I recognize both her face and her style.

I got sidetracked. But I am sure you will agree that the tangent was worth it. I was talking about Ghislaine having likely been responsible for the Atlantis symbolism surrounding Jeffrey, and the connection this may have had to the "model scouting." In this regard, it is worthy of note that one of Ghislaine's associates in the modeling world, British fashion designer Alexander McQueen, was "suicided" shortly after coming out with what would be his last line—"Plato's Atlantis." The clothing and accessories that McQueen designed for this line have an archeo-futuristic and transhumanist aesthetic that clearly calls to mind the mythos and ethos of the Belial group. Interestingly, the Alexander McQueen flagship store is only a couple of blocks from Ghislaine's Manhattan townhouse.

Whose idea was it to name Ghislaine and Epstein's submarine "Atlantis" (the one that she piloted) or to take scientists who specialized in subjects such as quantum gravity, robotics, cybernetics, and gene splicing down into the parts of the Caribbean where Atlantean ruins have been discovered? Who really instigated Jeffrey Epstein's visit to Cuba to meet with Fidel Castro after Paulina Zelitsky discovered that megalithic city hundreds of meters below the western tip of the island?

How interesting that, after finally leaving Jeffrey Epstein, the next man that Ghislaine gets seriously involved with is a certain Scott Borgerson, whose Cargometrics hedge fund based on shipping lane metrics is particularly concerned with the question of regulation, or the lack thereof, in the Antarctic. Did Ghislaine follow Wilson, Flem-Ath, and Hapgood, as I did, in considering that, despite having extensive colonies in what is now the Caribbean and the Bahamas, perhaps all the way up to the Azores, the Atlantean homeland may actually have been Antarctica? (Remember "A–17"?) Here is what Borgerson, who Ghislaine secretly married, had to say about the lack of regulations and the potential for resource exploitation in Antarctica after climate change-induced de-glaciation, in an article that he penned for *The Guardian*: "While at the top of our world sits the polar sea, at the bottom lies the ice-covered continent of Antarctica. As its ice cover melts this isolated continent will rise from the shadows like Atlantis transmigrating from imagination to reality."

Scott Borgerson helped Ghislaine to manage her TerraMar Project, which she launched in 2014. Many in the mainstream media have speculated that TerraMar was some kind of front or publicity stunt aimed at remaking her image after distancing herself from Epstein. I do think that it was a front, but not at all the kind of publicity stunt that these professional peddlers of disinformation would have the public believe. First of all, Ghislaine Maxwell has genuinely had a deep lifelong interest in the oceans. She wanted to be a marine biologist, but her father would not let her — insisting that she go into business, *his* business. That having been said, TerraMar *was* a front — for continuing her search for Atlantis and, potentially, for building a New Atlantis. It is this phase of Ghislaine's quest that became the basis for my vision of her, in *Uber Man*, as the project leader of Dana Avalon's NovAtlantis initiative.

Borgerson, whose profile fits that of a former Naval Intelligence operative, boasted that Cargometrics was aiming to become "the NSA of the seas." Detailed information on the movements of various types of vessels along all of the shipping lanes of the world would be very useful in determining just what sectors of the high seas were most secluded and ungoverned. Over and over again during her various speeches promoting the TerraMar Project, including nine addresses to the United Nations, Ghislaine Maxwell emphasized the lawlessness of the high seas, which make up no less than 45% of our planet. 71% of the Earth is ocean. 64% of the ocean lies outside the territorial waters, and the legal jurisdiction, of any one nation.

On the face of it, her advocacy for universal adherence to the Law of the Seas Convention seems to be geared toward ocean conservation and wildlife protection, addressing the tragedy of "the global commons" that no one in particular cares about because it is owned by no one and belongs to everyone. But what Ghislaine was really after, by pushing, for example, for the United States to finally sign the convention, was to make sure that as little of the oceans as possible were under the legal jurisdiction of one or another nation-state and, by extension, within the scope of enforceable international law. While lamenting the overfishing done by certain countries and corporate syndicates, Ghislaine's real aim was to keep as much of the high seas as free of regulation as possible. To preserve their outlaw status as the aquatic equivalent of the Wild West, a frontier for pirates of all kinds—including Promethean pirates.

If Maxwell has not read Carl Schmitt's *Theory of the Partisan,* then I wager that she at least understands his argument there intuitively, especially where Schmitt enters into the subject of "cosmopirates and cosmopartisans" of the future. It is at the margins of state power that the true nature of sovereign authority and its relationship with constitutional and international law can really be understood. Captain Nemo in Jules Verne's *Twenty Thousand Leagues Under the Sea* (1870) or Captain "Wolf" Larsen in Jack London's *The Sea Wolf* (1904) are figures that Schmitt could have used to radicalize his argument for how sovereign power, and the constitutional order that it produces, precedes, and is unbound by the legal system that it may formulate or dissolve. Granting that Schmitt was right that a law lacking any sovereign power to enforce it is no binding law at all, in international waters, beyond the enforceable jurisdiction of any nation-state, order still endures aboard the ships of outlaw captains. Ghislaine's intense interest in *The Outlaw Ocean* series of articles written by Ian Urbina of *The New York Times*, which was subsequently adapted into a book, is a clue to what she was really after with TerraMar and the value she saw in associating herself with Borgerson and Cargometrics.

In *The Outlaw Ocean*, Urbina writes: "The rule of law—often so solid on land, bolstered and clarified by centuries of careful wordsmithing, hard-fought jurisdictional lines, and robust enforcement regimes—is fluid at sea, if it's to be found at all." This is tremendously significant in light of the fact that "merchant ships haul about 90 percent of the world's goods" since "moving freight by sea is much cheaper than by air partly because international waters are so uncluttered by national bureaucracies and unconstrained by rules." In other words, a sufficiently powerful group of stateless pirates could, in theory, hold the population of the entire planet hostage by dominating or disrupting global shipping lanes.

In 2014, Urbina managed to convince *The New York Times* to send him on assignment aboard a ship called the *Bob Barker*, which belonged to Sea Shepherd, a vigilante ocean conservation group. They were using the vessel to chase after a notorious pirate ship called the *Thunder*. Ships like the *Thunder* rarely, if ever, go in to a port. They stay out at sea, sometimes a couple of hundred miles from any coastline, and are both refueled and resupplied by other vessels that do call at ports but are less infamous and are not known to have dealings with pirate ships. Sea Shepherd was run by Paul Watson, who had been a co-founder of Greenpeace, before being kicked out of Greenpeace for being too radical and aggressive in his environmentalist activism on the high seas. Sea Shepherd had a small navy consisting of ten ships, two drones, and 120 men and women with backgrounds from twenty-four different nations. Sea Shepherd's motto is: "Takes a pirate to catch a pirate." Urbina describes their chase of the *Thunder* as "a battle of bold vigilantism against persistent criminality." The *Thunder*, which also sailed under other aliases, was an illegal fishing vessel, whose true ownership was obscured by multiple shell companies in the Seychelles, Nigeria, and Panama, with some authorities suspecting (but unable to prove) that the Spanish fish-poaching company Vidal Armadores was the true owner. The illicit seafood trade is a business that rakes in $160 billion a year for the criminals who run it. One in every five seafood dishes served at first-world restaurants has been netted illegally. At one or another time, the *Thunder* sailed under the flags of the United Kingdom, the Seychelles, Belize, Tongo, and at the time of Urbina's reporting was alternating between flying the flags of Mongolia and Nigeria.

Pirate ships would sail under the infamous Jolly Roger or flag of the skull and crossed bones in the days when seabound vessels still only flew the flags of the country at whose port they were based or at whose behest they sailed. Beginning as a response to Prohibition (of alcohol) in the United States, from 1920–1933, which extended to regulations against US vessels even serving alcohol in international waters, a practice began of re-flagging merchant ships by paying companies in foreign countries for licenses to sail under the flag of the country hosting that company. These "flags of convenience" are, as Urbina explains, "cloaks of misconduct" that companies in third world countries are particularly eager to provide to customers who pay well. The governments of many of these countries, in Africa or Latin America, are also in on the corruption of these companies, since it is the country's flag that is being flown after all, as long as the state officials are given their cut of the corporate licensing profits. If, or when, Interpol comes after any one of these countries for such corporate practices, the companies revoke the pirate ship's license to fly that country's flag, and the ship's secret owners turn to another company in another country. That is what is behind the *Thunder* flying so many false flags. Instead of a proper port registry name and number painted on its hull, the *Thunder* had what are called "James Bond license plates" or a variety of different port registry signs that hung from its stern and could be quickly swapped. Finally, like all such pirate ships, the *Thunder* would sail with its AIS or locational transponder turned off so that it could not be electronically tracked by Interpol or anyone else.

For such vigilantes as the Sea Shepherd pirates that Urbina sailed with on board the *Bob Barker*, chasing and attempting to illegally "arrest" the crew of illegal fishing vessels like the *Thunder* is not just a question of the illegality of the fishing, but the ethics of ocean life conservation. Sharks are finned for shark fin soup and left to slowly die at the hands of other predatory fish as they sink to the ocean floor. Aside from the barbarity of this treatment, which I believe Ghislaine Maxwell was sincere in condemning when she mentioned it in all of her public addresses, sharks are a keystone species. As apex predators they keep the population of smaller fish down to a level that prevents the latter from eating too many of the microorganisms that sustain coral reefs. Consequently, poaching sharks and leaving them for dead ultimately means killing entire coral reef habitats.

Consider the case of Palau. Measured in square miles of land, the island nation of Palau is only about the size of New York City. 177 square miles to be precise. However, the chain of Palau's 250 small islands is so spread out in its expanse that the territorial waters of Palau extend the nation's sovereignty over 230,000 square miles, an area comparable to the size of Texas. Consequently, considering its small population and relative inability to defend its territory, the waters of Palau are a popular target for piratical fish poaching, including of very high-value seafood items such as Pacific bluefin tuna and Chinese sea cucumbers. At one point, Palau attempted, unsuccessfully, to negotiate a deal with the private mercenary military force of Blackwater to protect its waters. It is no mere coincidence that during one of her nine addresses to the United Nations regarding the TerraMar Project, Ghislaine Maxwell was seated next to the representative from Palau.

Gaining control of a relatively powerless but expansive island chain country like Palau would be tremendously advantageous to a large-scale seasteading project. Seasteads are to the new frontier of the outlaw ocean what homesteads once were in the largely lawless American frontier of the "Wild West." This is another subject that Urbina discusses in *The Outlaw Ocean*. Seasteads are platforms or other habitable structures moored in international waters; they could even be adapted out of large, anchored ships—such as cruise ships. For example, the startup "Blueseed" seastead that Dario Mutabdzija proposed to be built in international waters off the coast of Silicon Valley (at 12 nautical miles off the coast of California).

Urbina focuses on one particularly controversial seastead, Sealand, which also became a micronation. Located off the coast of England in the North Sea, just beyond British territorial waters, Sealand began as an abandoned 1940s British Navy platform with a helipad, built in Brutalist style, with an expanse not larger than two tennis courts, sitting on top of two concrete towers that raise the structure sixty feet above the ocean. In the late 1960s, it was taken over by Roy Bates, together with his family and friends. Initially, Roy used it as the base for a pirate radio station broadcasting pop music bands back into the British Isles. But by the 1970s, the Bates family had declared Sealand to be a sovereign nation, with its own flag, passport, coat of arms, embossed gold and silver coins, air mail stamps, and a motto: *E Mare, Libertas*, "From the Sea, Freedom."

Initially, diplomatic recognition was hard to get, and there were a few skirmishes between the Bates family and the British Royal Navy. The courts, however, decided in favor of Bates and Sealand, declaring that the United Kingdom had no jurisdiction there. But de facto recognition eventually came when West Germany was forced to send an ambassador to Sealand in 1978 to negotiate the release of a certain

Gernot Pütz, who was involved in a failed coup attempt organized by Alexander Gottfried Achenbach, the so-called "foreign minister of Sealand," together with a few other Germans. The fact that the coup plotters were thrown in the brig by a triumphant Roy Bates, and that Pütz was held there for two months, until the West German ambassador was able to negotiate his release for a sum of 75,000 Deutsche Marks to be paid to the Bates family, is itself an interesting study in the dynamics of constituting sovereign authority in a realm beyond the reach of any national law and forcing others to at least implicitly recognize this claim.

Over the years following this victory, Sealand's size may not have grown but its stature and reputation did, to the point that in 2010, WikiLeaks approached Sealand with a request to allow Julian Assange to take refuge there. Bates declined. At one point, a server company called HavenCo wanted to use Sealand as a site for secure servers, since seawater can be used to cool these servers just as well as the very expensive air-conditioning systems that are required to do so when they are land-based. Even Google has shown interest in building offshore data storage centers with seawater-cooled servers. However, as one can imagine, Sealand also became a nexus for global organized crime. Various crime syndicates, including arms dealers, began to forge Sealand passports—or at least Bates *claims* that they were forged—in order to secure diplomatic immunity, *or the appearance of it*, in various countries wherein their operations were liable to get them prosecuted. According to a story in the *Los Angeles Times*, Sealand passports were used by one group of arms dealers who managed to sell no less than fifty Russian tanks, ten MiG-23 fighter jets, and armored vehicles and artillery to buyers in Sudan for a sum of $50 million.

Sealand was located in a relatively accessible stretch of ocean, just outside of British territorial waters. There are, however, parts of the outlaw ocean that are nearly impenetrable by surface vessels. With two-hundred-mile-an-hour winds and ninety-foot-tall waves, the international waters between Argentina and Antarctica are particularly hard to navigate. A sufficiently robust seastead firmly moored in an area like this, perhaps with most of the structure extending below the gigantic waves, would be an almost unreachable lair, except by submarine. There is an old sailing proverb to the effect that "below latitude 40° south there is no law, and below 50° south, no God." Urbina goes on to remark that the outlaw ocean is not only "a cold and predatory environment… a habitat for the brutal exercise of evolutionary fitness…" but "also a place of discovery, of limitless aspiration and reinvention."

It was certainly all of those things for Ghislaine Maxwell. There is this great line that she repeats in most of her TerraMar speeches, about how she is a "speed demon" and if there were no traffic cops, she would be the one running all the red lights on the road. As I suggested in *Uber Man*, the regulatory objectives of TerraMar were meant to set the stage for the preservation of "the blue heart of the Earth" and the seabed, including subsurface mountain ranges and ridges of the high seas, for stealth colonization by "a new country," as Ghislaine often put it with diabolical tact. An outlaw nation. NovAtlantis.

The TerraMar passport gimmick was great. I find it quite amusing. Really, though, the only passport to the kind of country that Ghislaine was trying to create, out beyond any and every legal framework of the existing world order, was the passport of Promethean rebellion in the name of creative innovation, undaunted exploration, and intrepid enterprise. She may have been daddy's girl, but Ghislaine was no "Captain Bob." She was the Admiral of the New Atlantis. Or, at least, she *should* have been. But the Olympian overlords of this world couldn't have that now, could they? Ghislaine Maxwell had to be pushed into the clutches of Jeffrey Epstein so that she could be turned into a cardboard cutout, a dart board: "Madam sex trafficker." End of story.

No. It is *not* the end of the story. The ungoverned and essentially lawless high seas, together with the seabed beneath them, namely the

*Terra*Mar, or "earth of the ocean," are the matrix for the New Atlantis that the Belial group first sought to forge through its rebellion against the old order of an Atlantis still subjugated by Olympus. This is what was expressed for the first time in a putatively "fictional" form in *Uber Man* as the vision for a posthuman society being born from out of NovAtlantis — a cosmopolitan constellation of settlements in the ocean depths, where the Spectral Revolution and the Technological Singularity can be successfully navigated by a community with a cohesive, Promethean ethos.

The closest that any contemporary thinker has come to this kind of idea actually serves to underline how far the intellectual vanguard of today remains from fathoming it. Take, for example, *The Network State* by Balaji Srinivasan. What Srinivasan argues is that blockchain, cryptocurrency, and social media technology featuring AR and VR interfaces can spawn a new territorially non-contiguous and decentralized form of post-national political sovereignty.

The idea is that a blockchain-based network, operating on the deepest and most durable stratum of the internet, could serve as the fundamental infrastructure for a community of like-minded people who have their own cryptocurrency economy based on decentralized labor, production, and exchange, and who begin to acquire geographically non-contiguous territory in the form of real estate holdings in various parts of the world. Srinivasan thinks that once any community of this kind achieves a sufficient scale, representing billions of dollars of economic production or purchasing power, and millions of potential citizens spread across almost every continent, a new country could be formed by this community. He argues that most countries in the world are small in terms of the scale of their population, if not their economic strength. Some very small countries are quite wealthy, as a "Network State" would potentially be. Consider Luxembourg, Singapore, Switzerland, and Dubai (or the UAE as a whole). Srinivasan wants to believe that once a Network State (and there may be many such Network States) reaches this scale, it could secure diplomatic recognition as an actual sovereign nation, initially from a few individual countries that establish bilateral relations with it, and then, ultimately, from the United Nations.

The problem is that the United Nations is constituted by a constellation of sovereign countries, and at the level of the Security Council, its policymaking is predominately determined by the most powerful of these nation-states. None of these countries is going to be willing to recognize a new sovereign entity that is not only within its territorial borders, but that extends across the territories and borders of dozens of other nations and potentially across three or four different continents. As Carl Schmitt understood well, sovereign is he who has effective power over the decision of the use of force, even and especially when a constitution's legal norms are suspended (in a State of Emergency) within a given territory, as defined against another political entity by the sovereign's decision with respect to the distinction between friends and enemies of his nation-state. Srinivasan does not effectively critique this core of Schmitt's thought.

There is no way that any of the members of the UN Security Council are going to cede their sovereign power to communities within their respective territories that are claiming to have constituted their own country, but a geographically non-contiguous country that stretches across many existing nation-states. Srinivasan dismisses revolution and war as undesirable means of constituting a new country, but a revolutionary war is precisely what would result from the attempt of a Network State to effectively secede from any and all of the nation-states that its community extends across. Such a Network State would not be able to diplomatically secure recognition of its national sovereignty from the United Nations. Rather, it would find itself at war with, and besieged by, the United Nations. In fact, such a threat might be the only thing that finally brings the entire UN Security Council into lockstep to authorize the use of force against what will inevitably be framed as a global threat from a group of stateless rogues. Should the rogues of the Network State put up armed resistance, say from private security forces deployed in their own communities, the UN will frame them not just as rogues but as stateless terrorists.

To be sure, Srinivasan, with his background in Bitcoin and blockchain technology, is right about the nervous and circulatory systems of a future form of political sovereignty. To think along these lines with him, but well beyond him, something like the following system would be required as the basis for what he calls a "Network State." First, as an economic backbone, one would need a cryptocurrency that is based on the Bitcoin technology, and is interchangeable with Bitcoin, but forked so as to develop a cryptocurrency that is both fully private and also stable (pegged to the US dollar, or to gold, or to some abstract average of a basket of designated global currencies). Then, so as not to be dependent upon the existing international banking system or national regulation of marketplaces, we would need a Decentralized Trading Exchange (DEX) and an online marketplace, similar to eBay, but completely protected from governmental or corporate surveillance and interference. Transactions in this DEX would be carried out using the private stablecoin.

Employing blockchain technology and building up from out of the most durable substratum of the internet—the old ARPANET, built to survive a nuclear war, without any dependence upon the more fragile World Wide Web—this market would provide a framework for the exchange of any and all goods that might, for example, be produced by increasingly autonomous, private, and decentralized modes of production (initially 3-D printing, and eventually robotic nano-technological assembly). Obviously, such a system poses a very serious threat to established interests, not least of which is the international system of central banks and the control of both corporatist national economies (including Chinese Corporatism) and monopolistic multinational corporations over the world economy. It would, in effect, represent the emergence of an alternate and rival world economy. Consequently, an end-to-end encrypted communication system is also an indispensable component of this network. It would ensure that the members of the network are totally anonymous, and that their private information will not be available even to those who manage the network.

Srinivasan would probably be on board with most, if not all, of this, but where Prometheism parts company with his proposal for *The Network State*, or rather where we, as Promethean pirates, see beyond the naiveté of this technocratic proposal is when it comes to the effective control of actual territory. We could certainly establish a private security firm similar to Blackwater but committed to the ideals of our network community rather than being mere mercenaries for hire. In fact, the various and numerous clients of the DEX and marketplace who benefit most from the unprecedented anonymity and privacy of the system, as well as of its medium of exchange, would probably finance the development of such a security force. This force could, in the first place, be tasked with protecting seasteads that house offshore servers in various parts of the world. These secure servers would serve to broaden the nodes of the network beyond computers based in nation-states, and to thereby deepen the Promethean blockchain network's durability. The problem is when this defense force comes up against state power as it attempts to establish itself as the sole policing agency of the geographically non-contiguous "enclaves" (as Srinivasan puts it) of the Network State in various parts of the world.

Even those nations with the most serious conflicts with one another would likely band together against a collective threat to their national sovereignty on the part of armed and potentially "insurgent" separatists living, in some cases, on the territories of two or more countries that are otherwise usually on opposite sides of various geopolitical contentions. Unless the enclaves of the Network State are only tentacles of some more substantive and cohesive octopus somewhere, an undiscovered country for which they act as fifth columns in the midst of the world's extant nations, the situation would grow quite hopeless quite quickly. So, where would the head of the octopus have to be, then, for it to be relatively fortified in the face of what might become the first truly concerted effort of the United Nations (since its inception in 1945) to wage war on a global scale? Well, "the blue heart of the Earth," as Ghislaine Maxwell would put it. The high seas or, as per Ian Urbina, *The Outlaw Ocean*.

Here we have the ultimate reification of the distinction between land power and sea power, as it has been developed in geopolitical theory by the likes of Hartford Mackinder, Carl Schmitt, and Alexander Dugin. What none of these theorists have considered in their prioritization of land-based heartland powers over the projection of force by sea-based colonial powers (which are still somewhat land-based) is the potential for Singularity-level technologies to fundamentally alter this dynamic. The stateless outlaw oceans, whether on seasteads or in undersea colonies, are the best place for controversial research on transhuman technologies that the UN will attempt to prohibitively regulate. As I have often remarked in my writings (including earlier in this chapter), Carl Schmitt began to have an inkling of this in his final work, *The Theory of the Partisan*, wherein he starts to contemplate the implications for state sovereignty that would follow from a situation wherein space-age technologies wind up in the hands of stateless pirates. But Schmitt was never able to complete the thought, partly because he was already in his old age, and it would have meant nothing less than an inversion of his political theory, which older people are not prone to doing.

I also failed in my first attempt to extend Schmitt's thought with a view to Singularity-level technologies when I wrote *World State of Emergency* (2017). Granted, a large part of that work was structured with a view to the intelligence operation that I was involved in at the time (and ultimately, the target of). But still, the vision of an intercontinental Indo-European World State that I presented in that book is an affirmation of land power as the template for an effective global hegemon, a de facto world government, capable of tackling unprecedented challenges to humanity at large and the planet as a whole. That proposal was profoundly mistaken and misguided.

Instead, what is called for is the completion of a thought that I began to articulate in *Prometheism* (2020) and then further developed, again, in "fictional" form in *Uber Man* (2022). Namely of NovAtlantis, the Promethean world state, as the ultimate sea-based power. Actually, the embryonic form of this conception was already there in the chapter of *Prometheus and Atlas* (2016) titled "Atlas of the New Atlantis" but, with my involvement in the Iranian Renaissance, I got diverted in the wrong direction with *World State of Emergency* (2017). Interestingly, when I left the Iranian Renaissance, with the publication of *Iranian Leviathan* (2019) as a public critique of their ideology, I started heading back toward this sea-based idea. The kernel of it is there in my treatment of the Cilician pirates in that book. They were the first Promethean pirates known to history. The Belial group precedes them, of course, but has been occulted in "prehistory."

In *Closer Encounters* (2021), I went on at length describing the tremendous capabilities of submarine tunnel boring and engineering inside seabed ridges and undersea mountain ranges. Since at least the 1980s, it has been possible, at a cost of billions of dollars, to build entire cities underneath the ocean. If these cities were built beneath the high seas, then they would be on territory that is technically outside of the legal jurisdiction of any nation-state. The ideal zones would be where international waters overlap with the edges of the continental shelves, so that there is no significant pressure change to contend with in undersea colonies (with seasteads on the surface nearby). Even treaties such as the United Nations Law of the Sea Convention only reinforces the outlaw status of these areas by strictly limiting the offshore territorial claims of the signatory nation-states.

As already indicated above, this was the hidden aim of TerraMar lobbying for global adherence to the Law of the Seas. Namely, to define a negative space that would be outside United Nations jurisdiction, even further outside than Antarctica, where there are a number of treaties in place (albeit ineffectually) limiting territorial claims and resource exploitation. I propose now, straightforwardly, and without any pretense of fiction, what I envisioned in *Uber Man* as the NovAtlantis project, namely development of a protected space for persistent pursuit of the Technological Singularity and its attendant Spectral Revolution in the face of an inevitable attempt at regressively Traditionalist de-industrialization that will, on the face of it, be led by China and Islam, but under the auspices of the United Nations.

The answer to this is not an Indo-European World Order that would somehow federate America, Europe, Russia, Iran, India, Japan, and the Buddhist countries. Not only is that becoming increasingly impracticable, given the demographics and mentality of the majority of people in these countries, it is also undesirable as a path to a Promethean world order. Rather, our goal should be to forge a Promethean society that extends from fortified undersea cities carved out of seabed ridges and tunnel-bored sub-oceanic mountain ranges, up through the high seas via stealth submarines, some of which can remain submerged for up to 25 years at a time. Then, of course, we also need large cruise and cargo ships, docking at harbors under the false flags of various countries and front corporations. Eventually, these docking "harbors" could actually be offshore floating sea-steading platforms that are designed to rise together with the sea level rise that is expected on account of climate change-induced de-glaciation.

The enclaves of the Network State that Srinivasan envisions would then only be the tentacles of this octopus, which would help to secure safe harbors or near-coastal sea-steading platforms for the Promethean pirates of NovAtlantis. Dependence upon land-based industry could be offset through the use of Singularity-level technologies, such as robotics and nano-molecular engineering, to achieve industrial autonomy by degrees. A hitherto clandestine alternative energy technology that involves a modular and scalable mercury-thorium reactor is ideally suited to power sea-based vessels and decentralized seabed settlements. The basic components and elements of this system could easily be produced within the NovAtlantis cybernetic ecosystem, and the energy platform itself produces far more power than its production demands. It is even more viable, and cleaner, than nuclear fission or fusion power.

This does not mean that we would turn our back on nuclear weapons. On the contrary. One ace card that we have in a potential global war with the United Nations, driven by an essentially Traditionalist anti-Transhumanist discourse of neo-feudalism thinly veiled as post-industrial "back to nature" environmentalism, is that we could use strategically positioned thermonuclear weapons to suddenly melt both the Greenland and Antarctica ice sheets in order to precipitously raise the global sea level by a couple of hundred feet. It would be the rebel Atlanteans bringing the flood this time, as a weapon wielded against the minions of the Olympians, who unleashed such a deluge on Atlantis to punish the insurrection of the Belial group.

Most of the productive economic and industrial power of the United Nations is concentrated in the coastal cities of the organization's leading member states. Engineering this kind of global deluge, which we would ride out from beneath and from above the waves, would suddenly alter the strategic asymmetry of power between the increasingly regressive land-based old order and the sea-based partisans of Promethean progress into a positively posthuman future. If so-called "humanity" does not want to face such a catastrophe, which could result in hundreds of millions of deaths in less than a week's time, perhaps the United Nations ought to let us do our own thing in the outlaw ocean rather than bringing international armed force to bear in a "Global War on Terrorism," where the new "terrorists" are not Islamists, but Promethean pirates.

The idea of "Promethean pirates" first surfaces in a certain passage of the penultimate chapter of *Uber Man* where Dana Avalon thinks to herself:

> What if the best defense against an Olympian takeover of the planet is actually a fractious world with multiple decentralized nodes of resistance in the name of Liberty and Independence? What if the right model is not hemispheric superpower collaboration on a global scale, aiming at an eventual

> Prometheist World Order, but rather a movement modeled on piracy and partisan warfare? Prometheus was, after all, a pirate — the first and greatest of all pirates.

This was supposed to be the point of departure for the third volume. The present volume has been written in lieu of it and can be considered an even more dramatic conclusion to the trilogy, one that brings "fiction" back to "reality" by deconstructing both *Faustian Futurist* and *Uber Man*, in what is less and more than a philosophical autobiography.

Promethean Pirates was going to begin with Ghislaine Maxwell writing her memoirs in an office at the top of the Woolworth Building in Manhattan in 1913, looking out over Lower Manhattan. She is, according to her biological clock, 47 years old. Narrating the memoir as she pens it, we find out from her inner voice that she met Dana Avalon in early 1992, just after moving to New York City in the wake of her father's death. In very short order, Dana Avalon earns her trust through the display of certain stunning tech and abilities, explaining to Ghislaine that she is there to reset the timeline for a second time. Apparently, following the events at the conclusion of *Uber Man*, Dana Avalon realized to her horror that her son, the one that she was trying to raise with Cybele, was not the reincarnation of Nikolai, but of Adolfo von Seelstrang.

During the night of November 30, 1989, amidst a stunning UFO swarm over Manhattan, involving the mass abduction of tens of New Yorkers, Dana sacrificed her son rather than allowing him to grow up to become the *Führer* of the Fourth Reich. Cybele left Dana over this. Consequently, Dana's connection to Apollyon and the rebel Nordic underground was also severed.

At this point, as Ghislaine relates to us, Dana told her that she realized that it was necessary to reach further back in time to prevent the Traditionalist Olympian Imperium from rising to power over the ruins of the modern world. But before using the saucer that Johnny had hidden away (after travelling in it from Gotham of 2112 to New

York in 1977), Dana contrived a way to meet Ghislaine and convinced her to come along on the time-traveling mission.

They travel back to 1896 together, where they find 40-year-old Nikola Tesla endeavoring to develop the World Wireless energy broadcasting technology as well as a wingless type of electro-gravitic trans-medium craft, for travel both in the air and undersea, that could be powered by this system. Dana makes Tesla understand that she is a reincarnation of him from three lifetimes into the future and explains to him that there is a rival group, led by a certain Wilson, developing the same technology as him, but that they are further along and almost have this tech operational. She opens his eyes to the fact that J. P. Morgan was only volunteering to fund Tesla so as to be able to appropriate his designs for this other group, for which he was the principal financier. With difficulty, Tesla is convinced to join this group himself, with the ultimate aim of infiltrating it and redirecting its development. Nikola Tesla, Dana Avalon, and Ghislaine Maxwell experience the "mystery airship" wave of 1897 from aboard the "airships" themselves, with Tesla having become a key player in the nascent Breakaway Civilization funded by J. P. Morgan.

Through Tesla, Dana Avalon meets Sarah Bernhardt and the two of them get involved. Meanwhile, Ghislaine recounts how she managed to seduce Tesla, who had hitherto resisted erotic involvement with any number of women who were interested in him. In his early 40s and her early 30s, they become a power couple, with Ghislaine having the business savvy and socialite networking skills that he utterly lacked and that, in the original timeline, ultimately contributed to Tesla's undoing. Using emerging breakaway technology from the Morgan group, Tesla designs a Jules Verne-style submarine that becomes the headquarters for a splinter group within the embryonic Breakaway Civilization. These Promethean Pirates work to alter the ideology of the Breakaway Civilization from within, and to clandestinely assassinate certain individuals who will otherwise be responsible for pushing it in an Olympian direction.

They also recruit individuals who could help reinforce the Promethean, futurist trajectory that they want to set for the development of this Breakaway Civilization. Foremost among these is John Jacob Astor IV. Ghislaine recounts a mission of the Promethean Pirates wherein their Verne-style submarine surfaces next to the Titanic as it crosses the Atlantic Ocean on the night of April 14, 1912. They needed to wait until Astor is confirmed to have been aboard, both to send a signal to those in the Breakaway Civilization who wanted to assassinate him aboard the Titanic, while carrying out an Olympian ritual sacrifice, and also to render Astor indebted to the Promethean Pirates for saving his life. Ghislaine recounts how, from the turret of the *Atlantis* submarine, she watched Dana Avalon, with a shotgun and a Samurai sword strapped to the back of her wetsuit, using grappling hooks to scale the hull of the Titanic and singlehandedly retrieve John Jacob Astor, bringing him aboard the Atlantis by the predawn hours of April 15, as the Titanic starts to sink from having been deliberately rammed into that iceberg by an onboard agent of the Olympian faction of the Breakaway group. Astor joins the Promethean Pirates, and by extension the Breakaway Civilization, as a second major financier and stakeholder, thereby diluting the authoritative control of J. P. Morgan.

The next operation of the Promethean Pirates is to intervene in the Chinese Revolution of 1912. They work both in Denver with Sun Yat-Sen and on the ground in China, with their objective being to maintain chaos and prevent the rise of an orderly Chinese Republic. Achieving this objective involves the assassination of key figures in the military and political structure of Imperial China, who would have been central to the rise of the Republic of China. Eliminating them means that a disorderly China divided against itself remains in the grip of colonial powers, not just Britain and Portugal, but also and especially Japan. Early overtures are made to select Japanese to join the Promethean Pirates and thereby further shift the developmental trajectory of the Breakaway Civilization away from Fascist Nordic supremacy. However, all of this comes at a price. While Dana Avalon is working to build up Mongolia and Tibet into an anti-Confucian Tantric "Shambhala," assassins succeed in killing her as she crosses through the snowy peaks of the Himalayas.

It is at this point that the narrative of *Promethean Pirates* was to return to that office atop the Woolworth Building. A year after Dana Avalon's death, Ghislaine Maxwell has become the occulted leader of the Promethean Pirates. Both Nikola Tesla and John Jacob Astor act as her chevaliers and frontmen, in what is still a man's world. They set their sights on preventing the chain reaction of the First World War and on taking the Breakaway backing out from under the rise of National Socialism in Germany.

Fritz Lang and Max Ernst, both still in their youth, are summoned to the headquarters in Manhattan to work together with Hugh Ferriss and Frank Lloyd Wright on a massive Futurist and Surrealist propaganda campaign, rife with Promethean "World of Tomorrow" aesthetics. The campaign, funded by Astor and directed by Maxwell and Tesla, is aimed at a Prussia and Austria that are never to be economically devastated by a humiliating defeat in the First World War. Meanwhile, the group also opens a paranormal research division under the direction of Charles Fort, who commutes from the Bronx to the spacious offices atop the Woolworth Building for work every morning.

While this would have been an entertaining story, and it may go on to be in the form of a graphic novel and film adaptation, by the time I finished conceiving of it I had also come to a deeply disturbing realization regarding Dana Avalon. Before I go on to explain what that is, let me volunteer the following about how I came up with "Dana Avalon." I was pacing on the loading dock of a storage unit in Chelsea one day in 2020, when all of a sudden, I saw that future city overlooking the partially submerged skyscrapers of Manhattan again. The name "Avalon" came to me very distinctly. It is an interesting name for a future reconstruction of New York on higher ground, since one of the most widely known nicknames for the city is "the Big Apple" and "Avalon" means "isle of apples." Manhattan is an island, and so is the only part of Greater Gotham — in the Palisades — that would remain above the waters were the sea level to rise about 230 feet in the event that both the Greenland and Antarctic ice sheets melted. It is also interesting from the standpoint of the geopolitics of the Anglosphere.

As Carol Quigley explained at length in *The Anglo-American Establishment*, since 1945 the early revolutionary American antagonism toward the British monarchical commonwealth had been entirely overwritten by an elite of interlocking round tables of gentlemen, mainly from the United States and Great Britain, but also from Canada, Australia, and New Zealand. They went on to fully integrate their defense and intelligence structures, building both the Five Eyes and the Echelon systems together. In the event of the destruction of the wider Western World in a Third World War, perhaps coupled with other convergent catastrophes of the kind I have written about repeatedly, it is more than likely that the diamond that would come from out of the crushed lump of coal that was the West would be some entity consolidating all that could be salvaged from the Anglosphere. Especially if this were an entity that was attempting to defend the Futurist-oriented Faustian spirit of the West against a Traditionalist Fascism that would certainly turn the Catholic Church and the countries beholden to it into vehicles for its regressive Imperium.

Avalon would be an appropriate name for that Luciferian bastion, or for its capital city, where the legacy of Milton, Shelley, H. G. Wells, Aldous Huxley, Arthur C. Clark, Ray Bradbury, Sir Ridley Scott, Stanley Kubrick and so many other Promethean spirits of the Anglosphere would be preserved as a fount of inspiration. I also think that the French and the Francophone Quebecois would be the one exceptions from the Latinate Catholic world to be a part of "Avalon." From Jules Verne and Luc Besson to Jean Giraud (aka Mœbius) and Philippe Druillet, after the English-speaking world, the French have been the most Promethean and science-fiction-oriented people of the modern age. The symbolism of Avalon, the Arthurian grail mysticism, with central figures such as the sorceress Morgan le Fay, was as integral to Brittany and other Celtic parts of northern France as it was to Wales, England, Ireland, and Scotland.

Finally, the woman that I felt I was connecting to in Avalon, and through whose eyes I was seeing these precognitive glimpses of the place, was actually named Sofia. With a view to ancient Iranian ideas about the *Daena*, Sofia showing me Avalon became "Dana Avalon." I realized, in retrospect, that there was another 'reason' for the name "Dana" as well, which has to do with the life of Ghislaine Maxwell, and which I will come to before the close of this chapter and this book.

I changed the name of the city to "Gotham" because I did not want to affirm the ethno-linguistically distinct character of Avalon. I would not call it an ethno-state in the sense that I did not have the impression that the place had explicitly racialist policies, but my subconscious impression was of a place that was not as cosmopolitan as I would want a future "Gotham" to be. Of course, that is going to be a problem if it just so happens that the vast majority of the small minority of people left defending the "cosmopolitan" ideal in a forcibly regressed world dominated by Traditionalism happen to be people of Anglo-American or Franco-American stock. By the latter I mean both refugees from France to America as well as the people of Quebec following the disintegration of Canada and the potential integration of Quebec with Nova Scotia, Newfoundland, and what is left of New England, New York, and New Jersey.

My name change is problematic because it could very well be that the reason "Gotham" fails to make a stand against the Traditionalist Imperium is that, however Promethean it may be, Avalon is still too much of a land-based ethno-state. Reframing Avalon as Gotham may have obscured one of the causes of its fall. In other words, one of the reasons why, by the end of *Uber Man*, Dana Avalon is already thinking in terms of the approach of de-territorialized Promethean pirates.

The ultimate form of piratical de-territorialization would be a system that would expand from out of the outlaw oceans of Earth into colonies based both in the Asteroid Belt and also in the Oort Cloud. Readers of *Uber Man* will recall that in that "novel" there were repeated, albeit brief and cryptic, references to Asteroid Belt colonies that had become a refuge for Prometheists defeated by the forces of Traditionalism on Earth. As Gotham fell, the last exodus (of denizens unaware of Dana Avalon's imminent timeline reset) was to these colonies inside of hollowed-out asteroids in the belt between Mars and Jupiter.

In *Uber Man*, journeys to these colonies were from land-based spaceports, with the one in the Catskill Mountains, just north of Gotham, having been explicitly mentioned. However, in the event that Prometheism would turn the high seas and the ocean floor beneath them into the bastion of resistance against Traditionalism, we would have to be able to launch our spacecraft directly from out of the ocean. This is not as difficult as it seems. From 1999 to 2014, a multinational corporate venture named Sea Launch, combining the efforts of Norway, Russia, Ukraine, and the United States, successfully carried out thirty-two maritime launches of rockets bearing commercial payloads into geostationary transfer orbit. These were launched from a floating platform, called *Odyssey*, which could be self-propelled to the optimal equatorial launch latitude (unlike land-based sites, such as Cape Canaveral in Florida, French Guyana, or Baikonur, Kazakhstan, which are close but still not optimal). The project ceased only with Russian intervention in Ukraine in 2014, causing irresolvable problems between two of the principal parties to the corporate venture.

The example of Sea Launch is only meant to render maritime space launches more tangible and practicable, even with today's technology. However, with Zero Point Energy drives, trans-medium craft, which effectively function as stealth submarines underwater, could slip through the surface of the ocean and head to distant asteroids or even more far-flung comets without requiring such industrially burdensome and easily detectable launch platforms as the *Odyssey* (or much larger ones that would be required to send people into space instead of just putting satellites into orbit).

Of course, such Zero Point Energy technology would also make mining and colonizing the Asteroid Belt a lot easier than it would be in rocket-fueled zero-gravity spacecraft. Of course, ZPE-propelled craft have a local gravitational field, presumably set to 1G (Earth-equivalent gravity). Such craft could serve as the home for Prometheist cosmopirates while they ensconce any given asteroid with a nano-molecular mesh that hardens its structure from the outside, so that it retains its structural integrity as robots, brought along aboard the spacecraft, begin hollowing the asteroid out from the inside. The colony built on the interior of the asteroid would be constructed inside of a rotational structure that produces artificial gravity, with some kind of nano-molecular buffer between the outside of this cylinder and the rocky interior of the asteroid. Past this point, the major challenge would be blocking radiation that could, especially in the long run, prove very harmful to the health of inhabitants. But any asteroid that is at least 100 meters thick would already act as a sufficient radiation shield for the colonists within it.

These colonists would manage robots and largely automated industries engaged in mining other nearby asteroids for a plethora of minerals and gases that, once processed, would provide for their every need without any expectation of resupply from Earth. Everything from drinkable water and breathable air to a variety of exotic metals and meta-materials could be produced within the Asteroid Belt. In fact, mining and industrial processing of these asteroids could supply Prometheists back on Earth with a variety of goods that could make life in and under the oceans more comfortable and sustainable. This, in turn, would solidify our sea-based platforms for deep space exploration and colonization. The new motto of Prometheism, the motto of the Promethean Pirates: *De Profundis Excelsior*, "From out of the depths, ever-upwards."

For our Traditionalist enemies, based on planets such as Earth and Mars, or even on moons of Jupiter and Saturn, such as Europa and Titan, to find Prometheist colonies concealed inside of one or another of the hundreds of thousands of sizeable asteroids in the asteroid belt would be like searching for a needle in a haystack. Even remote viewing would not yield much actionable intelligence, since it would be very difficult to pinpoint the location of the asteroid that was being clairvoyantly described—no matter how detailed the description. There are too many others surrounding it in that vast and fast-moving orbital belt between Mars and Jupiter. (Of course, the locations could be leaked, but that would be a matter of operational security internal to Prometheism.)

This advantage of widely dispersed stealth locations is even more true of potential colonization of the Oort Cloud than it is of the Asteroid Belt. Named after the Dutch astronomer Jan Oort, who first inferred its existence in the 1950s, the Oort Cloud is a ring of comets with icy nuclei at the outermost rim of our solar system. These comets initially formed near the orbit of Neptune, and then, over long timescales, due to the gravitational influence of Neptune, they were pushed into the fringe of our solar system. We are talking about hundreds of billions of comets that orbit our Sun at a distance of anywhere between half a light year and two light years from Earth, taking a few million years for any one of these comets to complete a single orbit. In 1972, Physicist Freeman Dyson became the first scientist to suggest that it would be possible to colonize the comets in the Oort Cloud. Dyson went so far as to claim that these "small worlds a few miles in diameter, rich in water and other chemicals essential to life... are the major potential habitat of life in space" rather than planets or their moons.

ZPE propulsion would make travel to even the furthest of these comets from the ocean depths of Earth even more eminently feasible than conventional rocket-fueled travel to colonies on Mars. Oort Cloud comets contain water, oxygen, methane, carbon dioxide, ammonia, silicates, graphite, sulfur, nitrogen, and a variety of organic materials. All of this can be robotically mined and processed into a plethora of compounds useful for sustaining human life and maintaining the warp and weft of a society with Singularity-level technology. These settlements would be spread out over many such comets, the largest of them being on comets about 10 kilometers in size. The main constraint on mining and colonization of the Oort Cloud comets is energy usage, with the majority of serious engineering proposals suggesting nuclear fusion as the principal power source. With the deuterium and tritium being mined "locally," this is a potentially very long-term but still non-renewable power resource, one that might support a small population for tens of thousands of years. In light of the reality of Zero Point Energy, this constraint is, however, immaterial.

In addition to all kinds of robotic equipment, Artificial Intelligence would be indispensable to a project as complex as colonization of the Oort Cloud. All manner of Singularity-level technologies would be employed in the largely autonomous industry of cometary mining, processing, and manufacturing. Consequently, it stands to reason that these technologies would also be brought to bear in artificially engineering an environment suitable for human habitation, not merely with a view to survival and vital needs but considered from the standpoint of reproducing and even exceeding the experiential richness of life on Earth. That means going well beyond the production of artificial biospheres. Augmented Reality and Virtual Reality would undoubtedly be used to interconnect the inhabited space within the Oort Cloud, and to evoke an expansive horizon of human — or Transhuman — experience within a vast and fully immersive Cyberspace with a fidelity indistinguishable from what we now take to be "reality." This prospect raises a deeply disturbing question: how do we know that we are not already living in some kind of simulacrum running somewhere in this Neptunian netherworld? Is that also a conclusion that I was contemplating, albeit through a glass darkly, as the narrative of *Uber Man* emerged from out of my subconscious mind?

It is quite possible. What Dana Avalon showed me, and what becomes clear enough if one steps back to carefully analyze *Uber Man* in light of everything biographical that I have revisited and recounted in the present volume, is that my life has been adjusted. I mean in the sense of *The Adjustment Bureau*, a film that I found so darkly compelling that I wrote an entire essay about it that appears in *Lovers of Sophia* (Manticore 2017, Arktos 2019). That brings me to why it is that I did not write the story of the third volume, the synopsis of which was presented above. It is because I realized that "Dana Avalon" was a device for my subconscious to be able to work out and process certain deeply disturbing realizations about my own life. I could not come to these realizations on my own in a rational frame of mind, so my "Dana" (in the ancient Iranian sense of *Daena* as conscience or discerning inner vision) did the work for me. She mediated my retrieval of this potentially shattering information.

I am not going to spell it out for you. Edit Dana Avalon out of the rewritten timeline of *Uber Man* (albeit paradoxically) and see what alternate version of my life you are left with. When I wrote *Uber Man*, I had no *conscious* knowledge of the fact that Ghislaine Maxwell's personal secretary and highest-level assistant, who practically lived with her at the 116 East 65th Street townhouse from 2000 to 2019, and who, early on, appears to have been one of Epstein's favorites, was a young woman named Dana Burns (who also went by the alias Kim Burns, and later married to become Dana Burns Perry). In *Uber Man*, Dana Avalon is trying to remember for me what my life was supposed to have been had it not been adjusted, and to identify at what points it was adjusted so as to bind me and subject me to an ordeal akin to that of Prometheus on the rock in the eagle's clutches.

Adjusted by whom? By the same people who, as I explained in *Uber Man*, drew from hundreds of surveillance recordings of my phone conversations with Nassim from 2018 onward in order to produce a dynamically responsive Artificial Intelligence, with both my voice and my personality, and used this AI to call Emma several times back in 2003. Besides *The Adjustment Bureau*, the TV adaptation of *Westworld*, which is now in its fourth season, also comes to mind. Both *Prometheism* (2020) and *Closer Encounters* (2021) contain lengthy commentary on the connection between time travel and what might be called simulacra but would be more accurately describable as the re-programming of a quantum computational cosmos with an in-built capacity for archiving, and potentially reactivating, overwritten timelines.

A cruder example, but one that would also account for civilization-wide resets that affect not just the biographies of individuals but also large-scale architectural structures by remaking whole places and times, would be the Gothic sci-fi film *Dark City*. The vision of *Dark City* is also the one closest to a scenario where we are inside some Oort Cloud-based simulacrum right now. Meanwhile, Christopher Nolan's *Inception* may be the best metaphor by means of which to visualize the potentially layered relationship between second, third, and n-order "simulacra" in a nested computational cosmos. It is better than *The Thirteenth Floor* because it takes parapsychological aspects of cosmic quantum computation seriously. Cronenberg's *Existenz* is not bad either in this regard because, like *Inception*, it leaves open the question of the actual "technology" that is being used to manipulate personal experiences of these nested simulacra, with what appears to be the tech in question on one level turning out to be an artifact of the simulacrum as it has been projected from a higher or deeper level where other technology or techniques are at play. Cronenberg had already made this basic point about the spectrality of technology, and its shaping of "reality," in *Videodrome*.

Why do such narratives speak to me so deeply? Because I recognize their most essential formal properties, not to say their archetypal features, from my own experience. Ultimately, I am not even convinced that we ever left Atlantis. My past life memories of Atlantis have a strange quality to them as compared to fragmentary memories of other past lives. Almost as if Atlantis is not in the past but is a deeper or buried *now*. I do remember that at least certain Atlanteans would go into some kind of hibernation-type chambers and submerge into a very long dreamlike state, which we would have to be carefully and slowly revived from. Is this a memory of something like what goes on in *Inception*? If members of the Belial group had all of the advanced technology that Cayce attributes to them, why would we assume that they would not be able to construct some kind of Virtual Reality system?

Moreover, if the group's aim was to radically reconstruct Atlantean society and to put down a violent coup from old-guard conservatives, still faithful to the Olympian Overlords, then why wouldn't they use whatever technology of simulacra they had in order to run many different scenarios of how a New World Order could be forged? Isn't it consistent with the purported "mad scientist" ethos of the Belial group, and their position on the "things," to find out what particular path to social evolution against the grain of Olympian control is most effective in producing a progressive and free society? How prudent would it be to break the "real" Atlantis before knowing what the best plan for reconstruction actually is? Perhaps it is called the NovAtlantis Project. Perhaps the Promethean struggle is not a resistance against the Breakaway Civilization as such, but a struggle over the ethos according to which an inevitable breakaway of rebel Atlanteans from the Traditional earthly order takes shape.

Was the supposed destruction of Atlantis the beginning of the simulacrum that we are still inside of right now? Wouldn't the Belial group also want a way to test whether those presumed to be "people" *are* actually avatars capable of reflection, questioning, and self-determination within this simulacrum, or whether they prove to be no better than Non-Player Characters (NPCs), and are therefore "things" rather than individuals with personhood? Is it possible that, like Dolores in *Westworld*, this is something that we have done to ourselves? I mean we — the godless, lawless, and unbound. Is it all a test, a *maze*, that is meant to determine who belongs in the future after Man?

These questions are as dark as the stormy seas that lie ahead of us. They are liable to produce what Kafka called a "seasickness on dry land." But now, there's no turning back. Like Atlas, we bear the burden of holding up the heavens at the end of the world. As Promethean pirates wielding the trident of Poseidon, we forge on ahead. So be it if we are chased by the lightning and the thunder. Stay under. Our story is not over. Our Leviathan sails on through the dark night of time.

OTHER BOOKS PUBLISHED BY ARKTOS

Sri Dharma Pravartaka Acharya	*The Dharma Manifesto*
Joakim Andersen	*Rising from the Ruins*
Winston C. Banks	*Excessive Immigration*
Alain de Benoist	*Beyond Human Rights* *Carl Schmitt Today* *The Indo-Europeans* *Manifesto for a European Renaissance* *On the Brink of the Abyss* *The Problem of Democracy* *Runes and the Origins of Writing* *View from the Right* (vol. 1–3)
Armand Berger	*Tolkien, Europe, and Tradition*
Arthur Moeller van den Bruck	*Germany's Third Empire*
Matt Battaglioli	*The Consequences of Equality*
Kerry Bolton	*The Perversion of Normality* *Revolution from Above* *Yockey: A Fascist Odyssey*
Isac Boman	*Money Power*
Charles William Dailey	*The Serpent Symbol in Tradition*
Ricardo Duchesne	*Faustian Man in a Multicultural Age*
Alexander Dugin	*Ethnos and Society* *Ethnosociology* *Eurasian Mission* *The Fourth Political Theory* *The Great Awakening vs the Great Reset* *Last War of the World-Island* *Political Platonism* *Putin vs Putin* *The Rise of the Fourth Political Theory* *The Theory of a Multipolar World*
Edward Dutton	*Race Differences in Ethnocentrism*
Mark Dyal	*Hated and Proud*
Clare Ellis	*The Blackening of Europe*
Koenraad Elst	*Return of the Swastika*
Julius Evola	*The Bow and the Club* *Fascism Viewed from the Right* *A Handbook for Right-Wing Youth* *Metaphysics of Power* *Metaphysics of War* *The Myth of the Blood* *Notes on the Third Reich* *The Path of Cinnabar* *Recognitions* *A Traditionalist Confronts Fascism*
Guillaume Faye	*Archeofuturism* *Archeofuturism 2.0*

OTHER BOOKS PUBLISHED BY ARKTOS

	The Colonisation of Europe
	Convergence of Catastrophes
	Ethnic Apocalypse
	A Global Coup
	Prelude to War
	Sex and Deviance
	Understanding Islam
	Why We Fight
Daniel S. Forrest	*Suprahumanism*
Andrew Fraser	*Dissident Dispatches*
	Reinventing Aristocracy in the Age of Woke Capital
	The WASP Question
Génération Identitaire	*We are Generation Identity*
Peter Goodchild	*The Taxi Driver from Baghdad*
	The Western Path
Paul Gottfried	*War and Democracy*
Petr Hampl	*Breached Enclosure*
Porus Homi Havewala	*The Saga of the Aryan Race*
Lars Holger Holm	*Hiding in Broad Daylight*
	Homo Maximus
	Incidents of Travel in Latin America
	The Owls of Afrasiab
Richard Houck	*Liberalism Unmasked*
A. J. Illingworth	*Political Justice*
Alexander Jacob	*De Naturae Natura*
Jason Reza Jorjani	*Closer Encounters*
	Faustian Futurist
	Iranian Leviathan
	Lovers of Sophia
	Novel Folklore
	Prometheism
	Prometheus and Atlas
	Uber Man
	World State of Emergency
Henrik Jonasson	*Sigmund*
Vincent Joyce	*The Long Goodbye*
Edgar Julius Jung	*The Significance of the German Revolution*
Ruuben Kaalep & August Meister	*Rebirth of Europe*
Roderick Kaine	*Smart and SeXy*
Peter King	*Here and Now*
	Keeping Things Close
	On Modern Manners
James Kirkpatrick	*Conservatism Inc.*
Ludwig Klages	*The Biocentric Worldview*

OTHER BOOKS PUBLISHED BY ARKTOS

Cosmogonic Reflections

ANDREW KORYBKO — *Hybrid Wars*

PIERRE KREBS — *Guillaume Faye: Truths & Tributes*
Fighting for the Essence

JULIEN LANGELLA — *Catholic and Identitarian*

JOHN BRUCE LEONARD — *The New Prometheans*

STEPHEN PAX LEONARD — *The Ideology of Failure*
Travels in Cultural Nihilism

WILLIAM S. LIND — *Reforging Excalibur*
Retroculture

PENTTI LINKOLA — *Can Life Prevail?*

H. P. LOVECRAFT — *The Conservative*

NORMAN LOWELL — *Imperium Europa*

RICHARD LYNN — *Sex Differences in Intelligence*

JOHN MACLUGASH — *The Return of the Solar King*

CHARLES MAURRAS — *The Future of the Intelligentsia & For a French Awakening*

JOHN HARMON MCELROY — *Agitprop in America*

MICHAEL O'MEARA — *Guillaume Faye and the Battle of Europe*
New Culture, New Right

MICHAEL MILLERMAN — *Beginning with Heidegger*

MAURICE MURET — *The Greatness of Elites*

BRIAN ANSE PATRICK — *The NRA and the Media*
Rise of the Anti-Media
The Ten Commandments of Propaganda
Zombology

TITO PERDUE — *The Bent Pyramid*
Journey to a Location
Lee
Morning Crafts
Philip
The Sweet-Scented Manuscript
William's House (vol. 1–4)

JOHN K. PRESS — *The True West vs the Zombie Apocalypse*

RAIDO — *A Handbook of Traditional Living* (vol. 1–2)

CLAIRE RAE RANDALL — *The War on Gender*

STEVEN J. ROSEN — *The Agni and the Ecstasy*
The Jedi in the Lotus

RICHARD RUDGLEY — *Barbarians*
Essential Substances
Wildest Dreams

ERNST VON SALOMON — *It Cannot Be Stormed*
The Outlaws

WERNER SOMBART — *Traders and Heroes*

OTHER BOOKS PUBLISHED BY ARKTOS

Piero San Giorgio	*CBRN* *Giuseppe* *Survive the Economic Collapse*
Sri Sri Ravi Shankar	*Celebrating Silence* *Know Your Child* *Management Mantras* *Patanjali Yoga Sutras* *Secrets of Relationships*
George T. Shaw (ed.)	*A Fair Hearing*
Fenek Solère	*Kraal* *Reconquista*
Oswald Spengler	*The Decline of the West* *Man and Technics*
Richard Storey	*The Uniqueness of Western Law*
Tomislav Sunic	*Against Democracy and Equality* *Homo Americanus* *Postmortem Report* *Titans are in Town*
Askr Svarte	*Gods in the Abyss*
Hans-Jürgen Syberberg	*On the Fortunes and Misfortunes of Art in Post-War Germany*
Abir Taha	*Defining Terrorism* *The Epic of Arya* (2nd ed.) *Nietzsche's Coming God, or the Redemption of the Divine* *Verses of Light*
Jean Thiriart	*Europe: An Empire of 400 Million*
Bal Gangadhar Tilak	*The Arctic Home in the Vedas*
Dominique Venner	*For a Positive Critique* *The Shock of History*
Hans Vogel	*How Europe Became American*
Markus Willinger	*A Europe of Nations* *Generation Identity*
Alexander Wolfheze	*Alba Rosa* *Rupes Nigra*

Made in the USA
Las Vegas, NV
23 July 2024

92822576R00121